C000174147

CANNOCK CHASE PAST

Sherry Belcher

Phillimore

2001

Published by
PHILLIMORE & CO. LTD.
Shopwyke Manor Barn, Chichester, West Sussex

ISBN 1 86077 155 6

Printed and bound in Great Britain by
BIDDLES LTD.
Guildford, Surrey

Contents

To celebrate the life of Russ Sishton
Aged 18
30 May 1983 - 23 August 2001
A truly remarkable young man.
Remembered and loved forever.

List of Illustrations

Frontispiece: The winding gear, Littleton Colliery in 1994.

Acknowledgements

The following have kindly allowed the reproduction of drawings and photographs: Daniel Burford, frontispiece, 43; David Battersby, 4, 17, 18, 22, 23, 27, 31, 32, 34, 35, 38, 40, 42, 46, 56-9, 61, 62, 63, 64, 76, 81, 97-8, 103, 106, 117, 120, 123, 135, 143-4, 146, 154; Kelvin Belcher, 8, 30, 101, 124, 136; Mrs. Joyce Bill, 67-74; Jim Brevitt, 45, 109, 116; Cannock Cricket and Hockey Clubs; 121-2; CRO, Stafford, 24; Rose Devall, 53, 66, 82; Mr. D. Earp, 88, 89; Mrs. Susan Edwards, 37, 110, 118; Reg Fullelove, 60, 65, 95, 96, 100, 108, 111, 115, 125, 138, 139, 152; Ben Gammon, 1-3, 5-7, 33, 36, 39, 41, 44; the late Trevor Groves, 137; Ray Harvey, 131, 145; the late James Homeshaw, 16; Christa Hook, 25; Mrs. Yvonne Hudson, 105; Norman Lee, 47; Mr. R. Lycett, 140, 151; Marquis of Anglesey, 19; Mrs. Maureen Macpherson, 86, 112, 113; John Moreton, 20; Wilf Nicholls, 126, 155; Mrs. June Pickerill, 83, 107; Mrs. Rogers, 79, 84, 85, 87, 90, 127, 133, 148, 149, 150, 153; the collection of the William Salt Archaeological Society, 9-12; Stephanie Seager, 147; Chris Southall of Hednesford Town FC, 114; Mr. J. Walker, 55; George Wright, 99, 119. The remaining illustrations come from the collection of the late Mr. S.A. Seager.

Many people have helped to make this book possible and the author would especially like to thank the following. Firstly, Dr. David Brown whose knowledge of the Anglesey estate and the Chase Coalfield is second to none; his advice has been invaluable. Secondly, Ben Gammon whose meticulous artwork has very much enhanced the author's work. Thirdly, the tireless patience and enthusiasm of many others interested in local history, including: David Battersby, Joyce Bill, Geoff and Jean Blunt, Jim Brevitt, Mick Drury, Reg Fullelove, Clifford Hooper, Trevor Mcfarlane, Maureen Macpherson, Wilf Nicholls, Kath Perks, June Pickerill, Jack Sunley and Alan Thrupp. Thanks are also due to the staff at Cannock Library. Finally, I would like to thank my husband, mother, family and friends for their support, encouragement, patience and forbearance in equal measure. I promise that there will be no more books until I retire!

One

Court Banks Covert and Castle Ring

Any fine summer's day will see a steady stream of visitors to Castle Ring - and, with them, all the trappings of the 21st century: from the overcrowded car park to the ice-cream van and the litter. Today, for better or worse, the Chase and tourism are synonymous. But a return visit on a misty autumn evening is altogether different – quiet, remote, eerie, bleak. At such times it is very easy to experience a sense of just how isolated the area must have been in the past.

Evidence of prehistoric people in the area is very limited. Perhaps the best was the discovery, in 1910, of a Neolithic chipping-floor at Court Banks Covert, by the Redmoor Brook, near the location of Nun's Well. Less than half a mile from Castle Ring, the floor is a very rare example, in South Staffordshire, of a site where flint tools were produced. Over 600 specimens were identified, although only 28 items were classed as implements, rather than waste. Sadly, modern farming has destroyed the site. Were these tools made from flints found locally, in the Bunter deposits? Or were they traded from further afield? Possibly, it was a combination of the two. There are virtually no remains to say how or where these people lived, except for a report, made in 1917, of some ancient fire-damaged stones at Bose's Well, a spring a few hundred yards south of Castle Ring.

Castle Ring is the best surviving example of the Staffordshire hill forts. At over 760 feet, it is the highest point on Cannock Chase; for the Iron-Age people of the area it must have been an ideal site. Once it had been built and the land cleared, there would have been unimpeded views over the surrounding lowlands, including the Trent valley; the most likely route for those intent on trade or war. However, despite the impressive remains, its origins are obscure. A powerful midland tribe, the Cornovii, probably built and occupied the hill fort, but little is known about them.

It is a frustrating fact, for those interested in local history, that the Cornovii is a surprisingly obscure tribe. They were Celts and their territory covered what is now Staffordshire, Shropshire and Cheshire, with Wroxeter, according to Roman evidence, their capital. No names of kings or

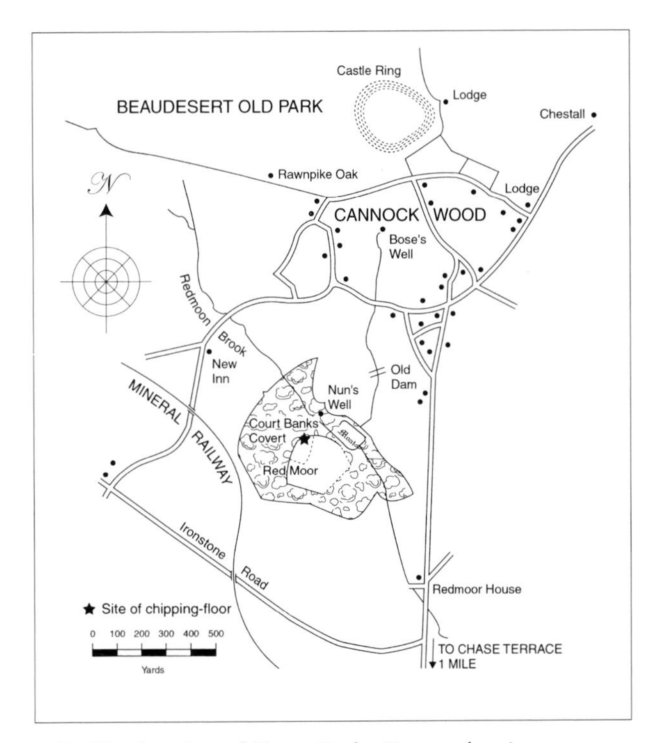

1 The location of Court Banks Covert, showing the position of the chipping floor. Flint pebbles are relatively rare and difficult to find in the Bunter deposits and some of the flints may have been brought quite a distance by traders or itinerant craftsmen.

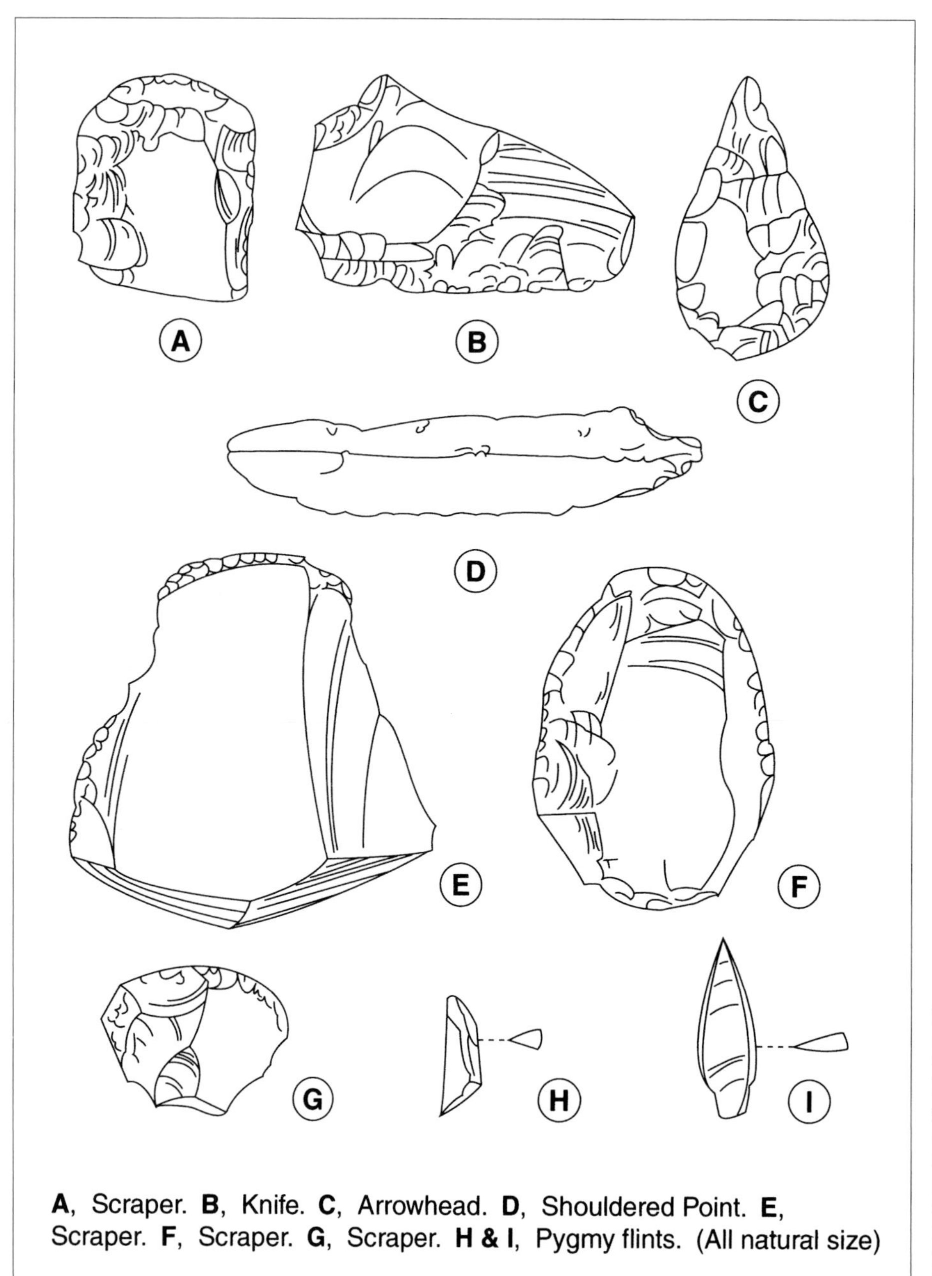

2 Very few – only 28 – complete flint implements were discovered at Court Banks Covert or nearby, and these are the best examples. Much of the rest of the material was described as waste. The finds were made between 1910 and 1916 by two members of the North Staffordshire Field Club.

chieftains survive, they did not issue coinage and no distinctive features of their culture remain, except the earthworks of settlements such as Castle Ring. The fort is roughly five-sided, made up of a series of banks and ditches designed to make good use of the natural features. The main bank or rampart, up to 18 feet high in places, protected the wooden round houses of the community. Timber fortifications and a wooden gate, guarding the only entrance, were almost certainly additional features. With all the benefits of today's technology, it is virtually impossible to imagine the generations of back-breaking effort that must have gone into its construction.

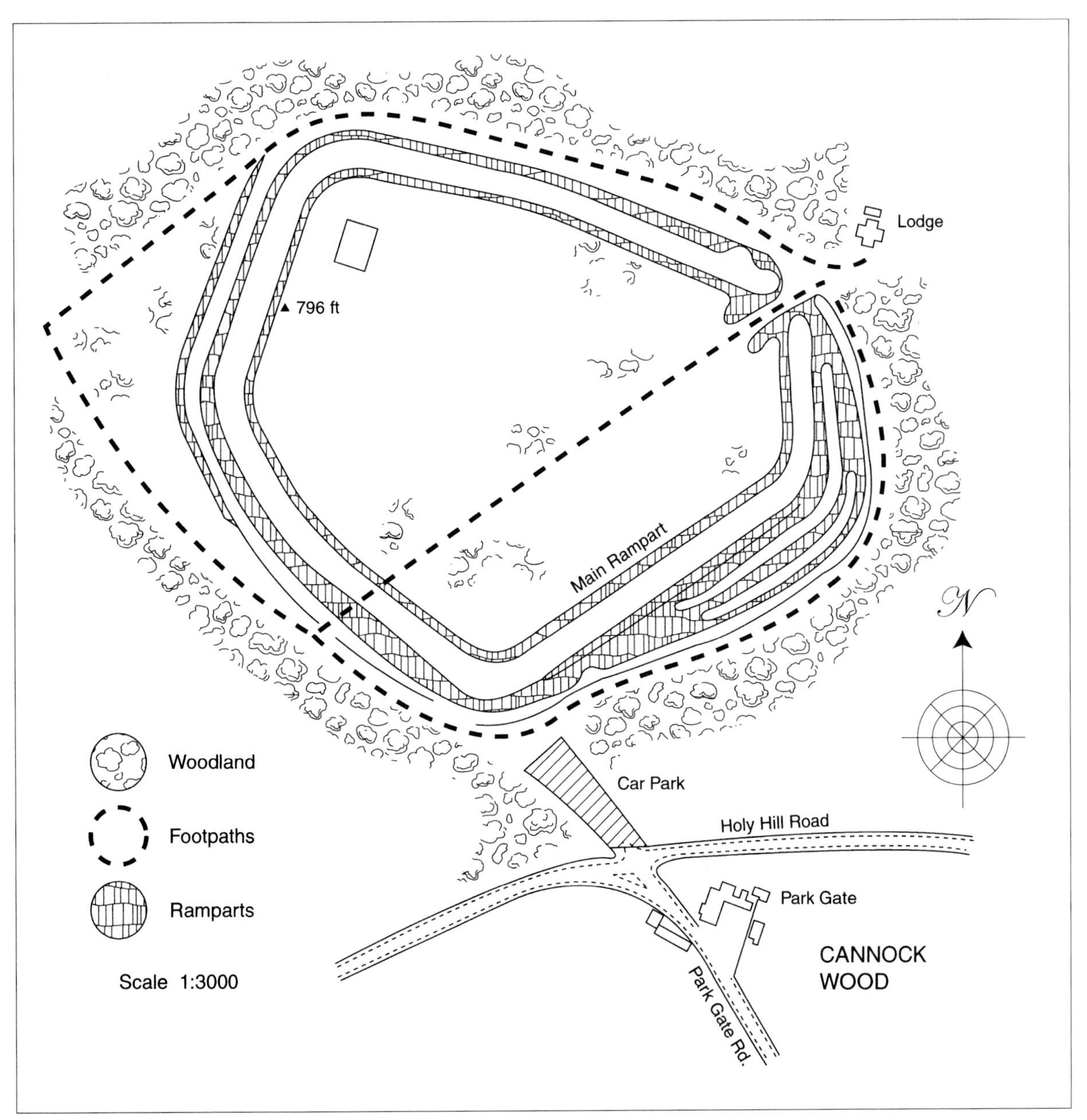

3 Site of Castle Ring, near Cannock Wood. Castle Ring is the best surviving example of a hill fort in Staffordshire. It is a multi-vallate hill fort, made up of a number of banks (or ramparts) and ditches. The main rampart is up to 18 feet high. The entrance, at the north-eastern corner, would have been protected by massive wooden gates.

Castle Ring provided a refuge at a time when tensions were high. It was a time of population growth and, consequently, pressure on the available land. Wars were more common than in what had probably been a relatively peaceful pastoral time during the later Bronze Age. Nevertheless, it was almost certainly much more than just a stronghold. Recent research has shown that Iron-Age societies were in the throes of massive change. Communities were becoming increasingly

4 A view of part of Castle Ring in the 1920s, before the surrounding area became a series of Forestry Commission plantations. Without today's trees it is much easier to get an impression of the size of the earthworks.

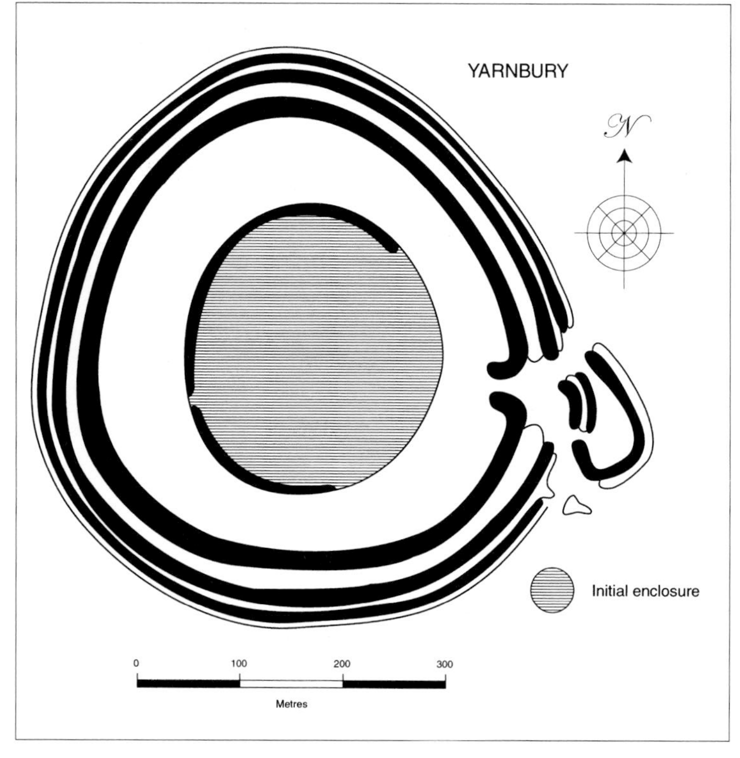

5 Yarnbury hill fort, Wiltshire, similar to Castle Ring in its basic design. The small inner ring represents the original defences which were later replaced by a much more extensive set of ditches and banks. It is now thought that later additions reflected the beginnings of a far more complex society. Hill forts became a symbol of the prestige of a community, as well as giving protection in times of trouble.

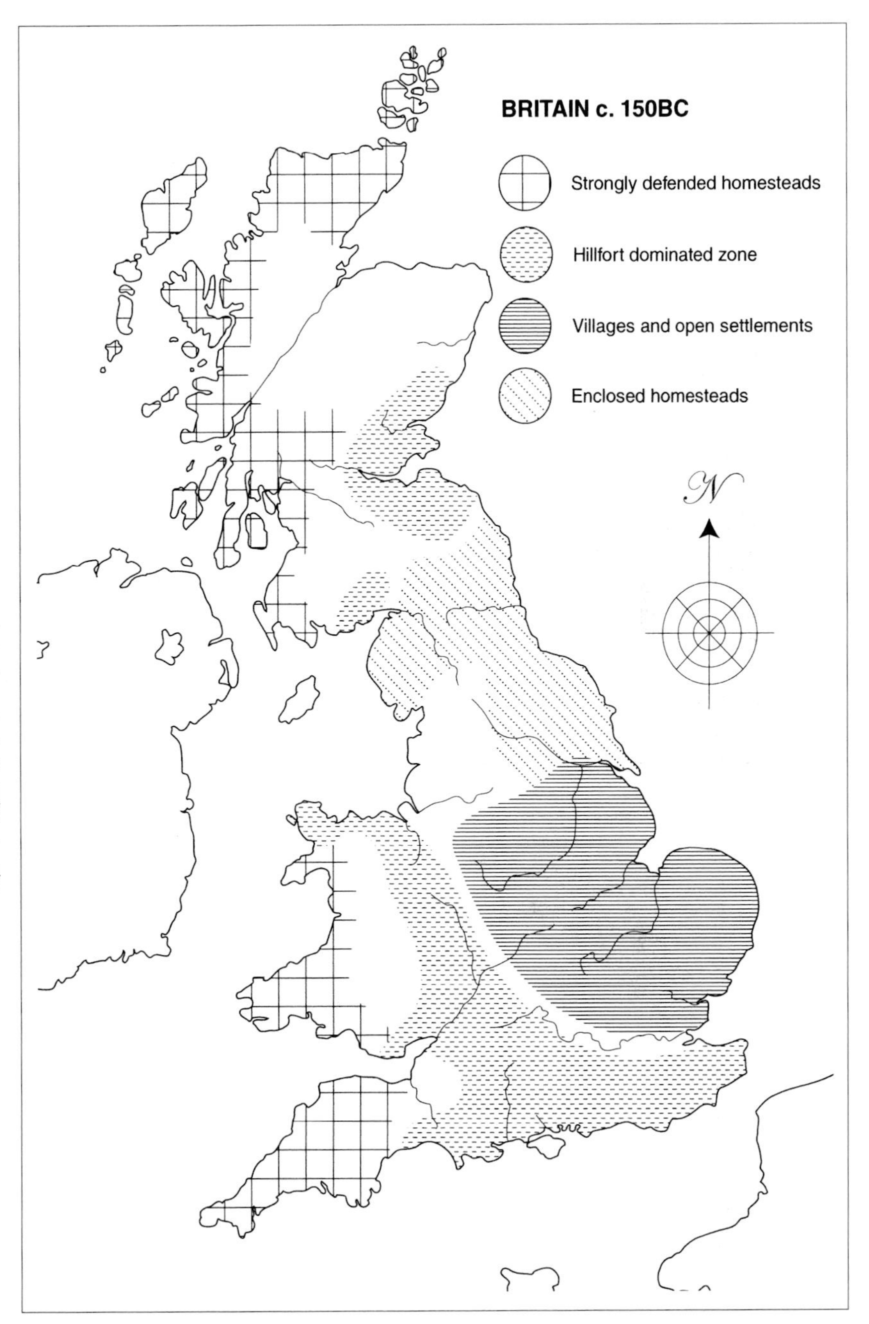

6 Hill forts dominated a relatively small part of the British Isles during the Iron Age. They probably evolved to suit the geography of the landscape, just as much as the other types of settlement patterns which emerged. The map shows a complex range of settlements, each with its own social system. Castle Ring stood on the very edge of the zone of hill forts.

sophisticated and organised; societies were slowly evolving from tribes to states. There is no reason to think that the people of the Chase were an exception. Thus, Castle Ring would have served as an administrative centre and a meeting place, as well as a fort.

It may be that the high ground of the Ring gave Cannock its original name. 'Gnoc' or 'Cnoc' is Celtic for 'high place'. The etymology of 'Cannock' is anyone's guess but 'high place' is less fanciful than some suggestions. Amateur historians in the past were often adept at making

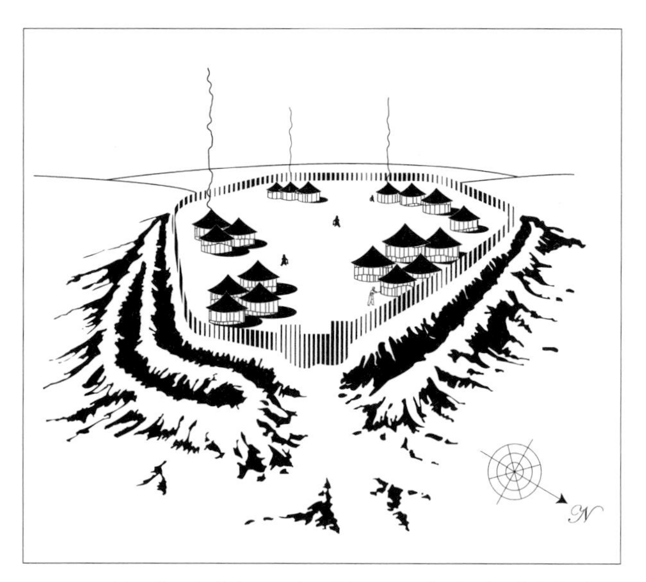

7 Castle Ring as it might have looked *c*.150 B.C. It was built around 500 B.C. The round houses were between 20-40 feet across. Most of the inhabitants would have been engaged in agriculture, but specialist craftsmen would have probably produced pottery, textiles and metal goods.

the wildest assertions on the flimsiest evidence. In 1593 Sampson Erdeswick of Sandon stated that 'Canke-Wood' should be called 'Canutus Wood'– or, Canute's Wood – simply because the king may have hunted locally. By 1820 a Dr. Harwood said the name derived from two Saxon words 'Cann' and 'Aig' meaning powerful oak. Cannock appears as 'Chenet' in Domesday Book and by the 15th century it had also been written as: Cnot, Canot, Chenot, Chnot, Chnoc, Canoc, Canok, Kannock, Kanek, Kanec, Kanochesbur and Cank.

Such confusion was no doubt due to errors by scribes and local voices grating on foreign ears. We often read that spelling was far more fluid in the past and did not matter so much. But this was not always the case. Careless spelling is a lawyer's dream! In 1313 Robert of Huntyndon (Huntington) sued the Bishop of Lichfield for depriving him of a common pasture in Canok. The bishop pleaded that the land was in Cannok and not Canok, and the suit was dismissed. So much for common sense!

8 Castle Ring today. Castle Ring can be seen at its best on an early summer morning, before the visitors arrive. A series of paths lead around the ramparts and across the fort. Several vantage points provide some fine views of the surrounding countryside.

Two

Romans, Saxons and Danes

The sense of the remoteness of Cannock Chase would have lessened with the arrival of the Romans, soon after A.D. 47. We can only guess at the impact of the construction of the Watling Street, cutting its way through the region. Whether or not it was built along an earlier trackway, the Roman road represented state of the art technology in terms of ease of travel and speedy communication. All sorts of artefacts have been discovered along the line of what is now the A5, although little evidence has come to light on the Chase itself. Rumours persist of Roman coins being found near the old Cross Keys farm, along with some sort of a mosaic floor buried deep under what was the farm yard. If they

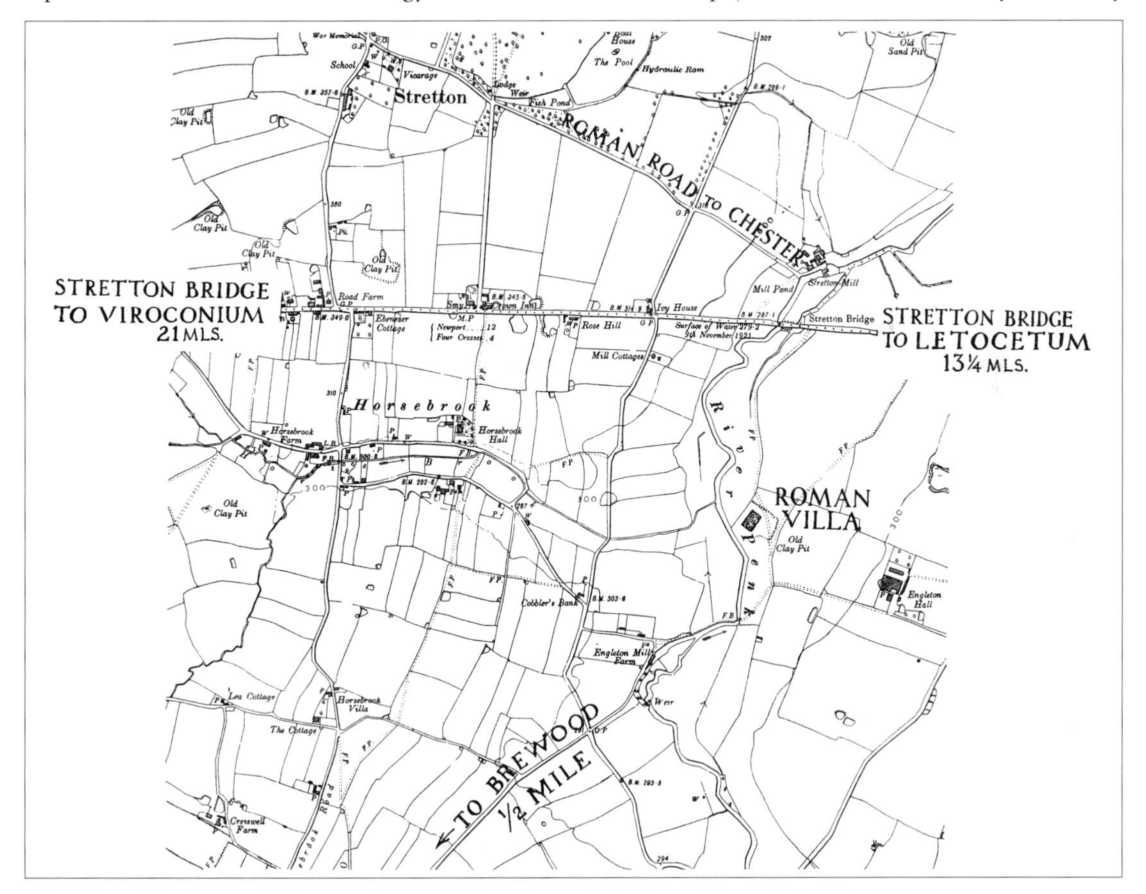

9 Site of the Roman Villa, near Stretton Bridge. It was built about 500 yards from the Watling Street and near to where the Roman Road to Deva (Chester) branches off to the north. The villa was built on rising ground overlooking the River Penk. When it was first built it would have been surrounded by open woodland.

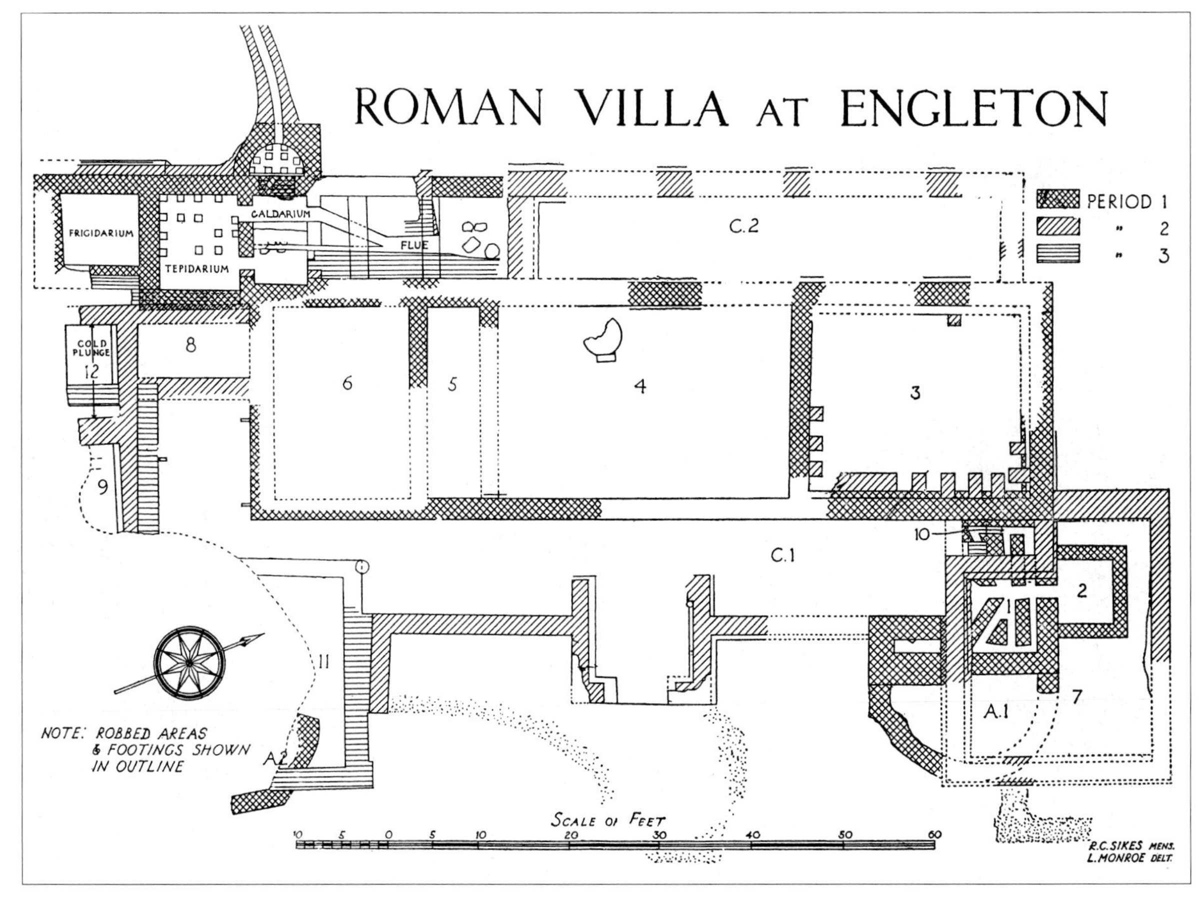

10 Plan of the Roman Villa at Engleton. The site was inhabited for several hundred years and the villa was rebuilt at least twice. It was obviously a sophisticated home which belonged to a rich and influential person, either a Roman magistrate or a Celtic chief who appreciated the benefits of civilisation.

are true, the original settlement of Old Hednesford could claim to have a longer history than most communities in the area.

The nearest tangible Roman remains lie at Wall (Letocetum) and south of Penkridge (Pennocrucium). Both are on, or near, the Watling Street and both developed as civilian settlements. As communities such as these began to flourish so the hill forts were abandoned; they had lost their purpose. The centralised power of the Romans, along with their rapid and effective communication systems, and their military might, made the likes of Castle Ring obsolete.

Pennocrucium was originally a camping station on the Watling Street, sited near what is now Stretton Bridge; a 13-mile march from Wall and a further 21 miles to Wroxeter. The station would have guarded the bridge crossing the River Penk. Also nearby was the original Roman road, running from Stretton to Chester. The only known building linked with Pennocrucium is a substantial villa lying about 500 yards south of the Watling Street. Luckily, it was discovered just as the site was about to be quarried. It was built of local red sandstone, but the dark grey roofing tiles probably came from the Welsh borders, around Ludlow. Sited just above the River Penk, in open woodland, on well-drained soil, it must have been a very pleasant and substantial home. It may have been the home of the local Roman magistrate, responsible for the civil administration of the area, but it is just as likely to have been the property of a local Celtic chief who had adopted Roman ways.

11 This general view of the villa shows very well preserved remains which, sadly, were reburied shortly after the excavations ended. It is to be hoped that one day a 'Time Team' might re-visit the site as there are very few known examples of Romano-British villas in the Midlands.

Whoever owned it enjoyed all the refinements associated with a Roman villa: painted plastered walls, underfloor heating and a range of bathing rooms. It was extended and improved at least twice. Locally, it is a very important site because, although there are more than 500 known sites of Romano-British villas, there are very few in the Midlands. The diagrams and photographs give some idea of the site that was, unfortunately, reburied soon after the excavations in 1937.

By A.D. 79, what is now England and Wales was firmly under Roman occupation. It would appear that local people survived relatively unscathed, unless the Roman historian, Tacitus, deliberately chose to omit the details. And this is possible, as it is known that he wrote favourably about the exploits of his father-in-law, Agricola, at the expense of other generals in Britain. However, there is no archaeological evidence of fighting around Castle Ring, unlike the battle for Maiden Castle, in Dorset.

The area was entering the next stage of its history. During the occupation there was anything between 40,000 and 60,000 Roman troops stationed in Britain. They came from all over the Empire – France, Spain, Eastern Europe, Turkey, North Africa and, of course, Italy itself. Those who were lucky enough to survive were rewarded with a grant of land and the gift of citizenship. Such legionaries were stationed at Wall and other relay stations along the Watling Street. Many must have settled within walking distance of such outposts, including the

12 The north wing of the villa. The wing was heated by a channel hypocaust running under the floor. It included the tepidarium, frigidarium and the caldarium (the warm, cold and hot bathing rooms). It was probably the first proper bathroom, belonging to a private home, ever built in what became Staffordshire.

13 The Watling Street at Longford Island. It entered Staffordshire at what is now Fazeley near Tamworth. It ran north-west to Wall (Letocetum) and along to Stretton, just south of Penkridge (Pennocrucium). It then went on to Wroxeter (Uriconium) and beyond.

lower parts of the Chase, when their time came to retire. They, and their descendants, were to enjoy 300 years of relative peace and prosperity. But nothing lasts for ever!

The raids on Britain by tribes such as the Angles and Saxons, which began in A.D. 367, must have been terrifying; especially as the once war-like Iron-Age tribes had been forbidden to have weapons for three centuries. By A.D. 410 the regular army had gone. Imperial currency became scarce and the once flourishing economy declined, along with the quality and availability of goods such as pottery and window-glass. The villas of the wealthier Romano-British farmers and merchants decayed. Everything appears to have gradually run down. Eventually, only the Watling Street remained – a lifeline, along with the even older trackways such as Blake Street, for the area, which reverted to an isolated, remote region, far from the main centres of population and activity, such as London and the south-east.

The end of the Roman era and the beginning of Anglo-Saxon England cannot be dated precisely. The Picts, Scots and Saxons had already made attacks on the frontiers of Roman Britain before the final withdrawal in 410. The earliest account of what happened after the Roman withdrawal was written by Gildas, around 550. Although lacking in many details and often inaccurate on dates, names and events, it paints a grim picture of raids, civil wars, famine and plagues. Gildas tells of the invitation to 'three shiploads of Saxons' who were given land in Eastern Britain in return for military services. What Gildas does not say is that Saxon settlement in parts of Britain had already begun in the fourth century, before the Romans left.

At the same time as Gildas was writing, the kingdom of Mercia, centred on the upper and middle Trent, was beginning to take shape; in the process the remnants of British tribes were being pushed further into Wales. There is no record, oral or written, of how this happened. The English Midlands seem to have been settled by a large number of independent groups, each with its own leader. One group, the Mierce (men of the March or frontier), settled in the valley of the upper Trent. Gradually they became predominant and by 650 Middle England had become the Kingdom of Mercia, and a formidable force. Ordinary people

14 St Chad, one of the first bishops of the Mercians, who established the see at Lichfield. Chad was a monk from Northumbria who was invited by King Wulfhere to become bishop in 669. He died in 672. His shrine became an important centre of pilgrimage in the medieval times. The see acquired large tracts of land across the Chase.

might have had new political masters, but the hard daily grind of life, based around subsistence agriculture, hardly changed at all.

Historians now believe that changes in agriculture were very gradual and that the move towards cereal growing had already begun in the late Romano-British period, rather than with the arrival of the Anglo-Saxons. It is now recognised – and makes far more sense – that patterns of agriculture are determined more by topography, physical geography and farming technology than by differences of race. Saxons settling on the Chase would have continued with mixed agriculture – grazing animals, especially sheep, on the poorer heathlands, which had been cleared for timber, and growing crops in the valleys. On the Chase the evidence points to a settlement pattern of isolated farmsteads as opposed to nucleated villages. The area covering what is now Littleworth, Rawnsley, Wimblebury and Heath Hayes is a good example. Any map produced before 1870 will show a series of isolated farms – but virtually nothing else.

With the Anglo-Saxons came increased servitude: peasants were drawn into a web of economic dependence, and then judicial dependence, as kings gave lords the right to conduct private courts. These factors came about with the impact of taxation, the demand for military service and the need for common protection during the wars with the Danes. The seeds of this system had probably existed from earliest times but it had become more organised, controlled and formalised by the end of the ninth century. The feudal system was evolving.

Christianity was another force for change during this time. St Chad (Ceadda in Old English) became the bishop of Mercia in 669 and was the first to have his see at Lichfield. An Anglo-Saxon, born in Northumbria, he had spent time in Ireland before becoming abbot of Lastingham and then bishop of York. With such a wealth of experience it is small wonder that he put Lichfield on the map as a centre of early Christianity. He died in 672 and was buried near the church of St Mary, which is probably the site of the present cathedral.

The foundation of the see of Lichfield would not have been possible without the support of the King Wulfhere of Mercia who had given Chad's predecessor, St Wilfred, generous grants of land, which included Lichfield. Some of these grants may even have included those listed in the Domesday Book of 1086; if this is so then the cathedral had connections with the people of the Chase from its inception.

The kingdom of Mercia lasted until the 870s when it was overrun by the Scandinavian 'Great Army', led by the Viking brothers Halfdan and Ingwaer. They, in turn, were defeated by Alfred the Great in 878. Again local folk had to struggle through these troubled times as best they could. By the reign of Cnut (1016-1035), Mercia had become an earldom led by Leofric. But this was short-lived and only lasted until just after the Norman Conquest, when it was 'all change' again.

Three

From Royal Forest to Bishop's Chase

The earldom of Mercia was one of the strongest in England in 1066. However, Earl Algar (or Alfgar) and his men were no match for the Normans, and Algar's lands were soon ceded to King William. Across the country Saxon lords were replaced by Norman opportunists, and the feudal system tightened its grip. For ordinary folk the daily grind, often miserable and uncertain, must have continued much as it had before. But the subdued country did not give up easily and William spent the first part of his reign dealing with rebellions and unrest. The years 1069-70 were some of the worst. A campaign of brutal repression that wreaked havoc across the country occurred in 1069 when William marched northwards to suppress an uprising at York. The following year parts of eastern England were attacked by Danes. To make matters worse there was a widespread famine as well. It was to be another 16 years before William felt secure enough to order a comprehensive survey of his realm.

The Saxon Chronicle records that in 1085

> ... the King had deep speech with his counsellors ... and sent men out ... to each shire ... to find out ... what or how much each landowner held ... in land and livestock, and what it was worth.

Not that the settlements of Cannock, Huntington, Hatherton, Norton (Canes), Wyrley and Rugeley, all listed in the book, were worth much. Some, such as parts of Wyrley, Norton Canes and Huntington were 'waste', giving no income, whilst the King's lands in Cannock yielded an annual income of 20 shillings. Nearby, Rugeley was valued at 30 shillings and Hatherton at 10 shillings. This pattern of low values is repeated across what was then Staffordshire, and the general standard of prosperity was low. In the upland areas of Staffordshire, such as Cannock Chase, it was at its lowest.

The people listed in the Domesday survey of 1086 would have had no idea of its subsequent value and importance to historians. The record is unique in the annals of medieval European history. According to one contemporary bishop, the record was made so that 'every man should know his right and not usurp another's'. Despite its errors and omissions, it is a wonderful record of 'Old English society under new management'. And without it far less would be known about the medieval landscape and English society. In it Cannock is described as a manor for the first time. Cultivated farmland supposedly extended to one hide, enough for 15 ploughs. Eight villagers and three smallholders worked three more ploughs. The surrounding woodland was '4 leagues wide and 6 leagues long' – about 6 miles by 9 miles.

Some words of warning! The stated extent of land holdings is rarely accurate. Firstly, much of the vast forest of Cannock is not recorded in Domesday Book. Only later medieval records show that the forest existed at all, as a hunting preserve; an area subject to forest laws. Secondly, the book records land in the area measured in hides and carucates – both supposedly 120 acres. Land in England had been 'measured' in hides possibly as early as the seventh century. The alternative 'carucate' came with the Danes. Rather than an exact measurement of agricultural land a hide is more likely to have been an estimate of value for tribute, or taxation purposes. Thirdly, there was a high proportion of waste villages in Staffordshire (some 65 or one-fifth), including local ones. Possibly the rebellion of 1069 saw their destruction but it is just as likely that, on the Chase, it was land deliberately taken back by the Crown within the boundaries of the royal forest.

15 The 'Beggar's Oak', an ancient tree which stood in Bagot's Park, Blithfield. Trees such as this were part of the great primeval forest which covered much of the Midlands. The forest laws of the Normans helped to preserve the woodlands against encroachment.

It is virtually impossible to estimate the extent of these wastes.

Most of the lesser landholders were numbered rather than named. The exception is Aelfric, classed as a 'king's thane', who held one carucate of land at Cannock, valued at 5 shillings. Cannock does not have many claims to fame at this time but in one respect it is unusual because its land is recorded both in hides and carucates. Why? There is no certain answer. However, Staffordshire was very much a border area between the Danes and the Saxons. In Derbyshire the carucate was the normal unit, to the south and west it was the hide. Perhaps the dual records reflect the area's uneasy past as a frontier zone, marked by the Watling Street.

One piece of land in Cannock, about 12 acres (a virgate), has a long and detailed history. From around 1236 one Robert Trumwyn held the land from the king. The Trumwyns must have been an important family as they held land at Cheslyn Hay and Hednesford as well. Robert's land passed through six generations and ten different owners by 1399, a stark reminder of just how precarious

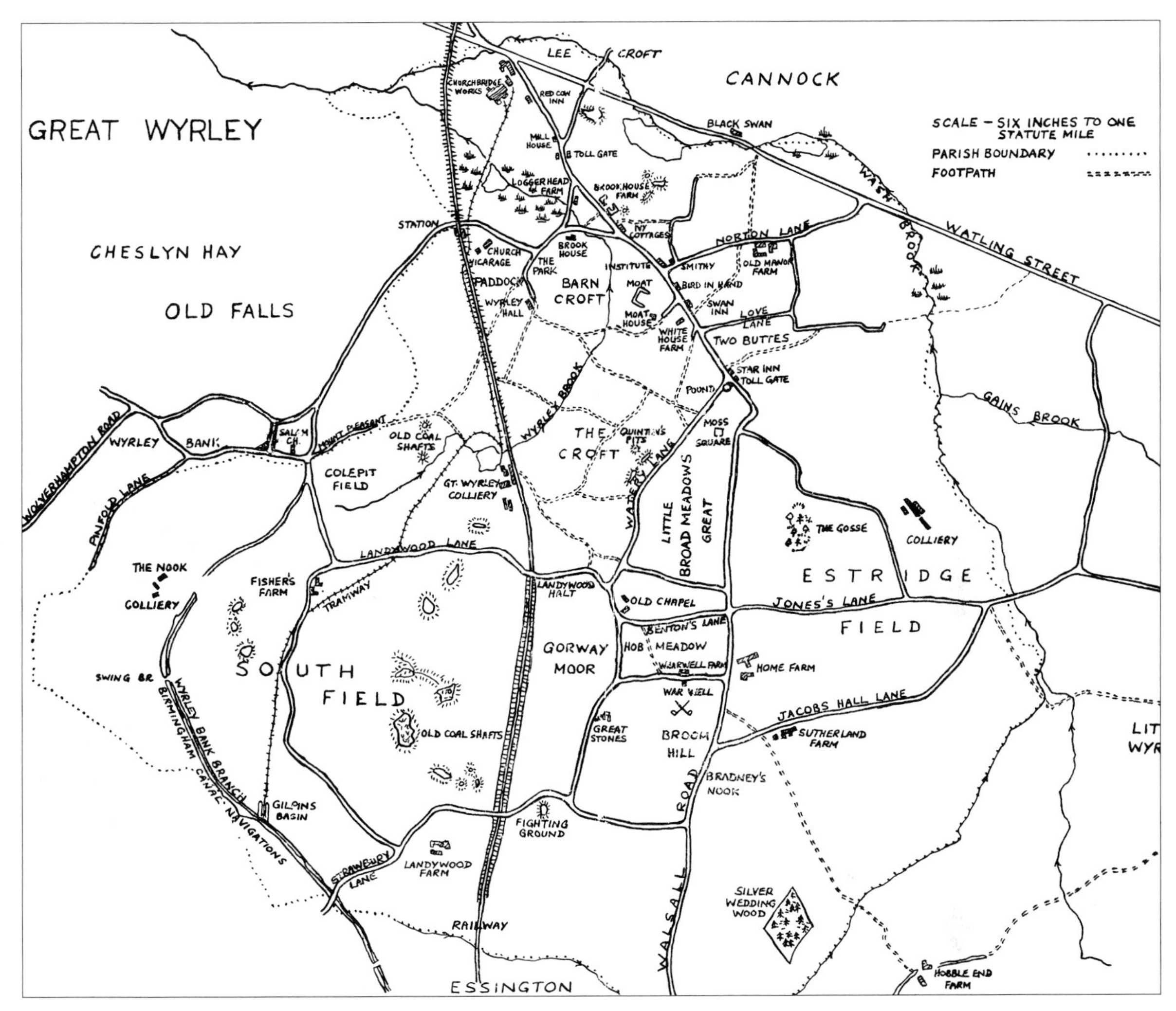

16 Evidence of the medieval open field system which operated at Great Wyrley. Note the names: Estridge Field, South Field and Broadmeadows. Today, Estridge Lane and Broadmeadow Lane are modern reminders of times past. This sketch was made by James Homeshaw in 1951 and was published in his book *Great Wyrley 1051-1951.*

life was then. Another branch of the Trumwyms, of 'Edensford', owned a plot of land called 'le Plash' in 1352, which is probably now part of Hednesford Football Club's new ground.

In 1293 a William Trumwyne of Cannock was listed as a knight on an assize roll. The family also produced Roger Trumwyne, an MP, who sat in Parliament in Lancaster in 1313. The Trumwynes were important enough to leave written records of one sort or another. One, made in 1349, provides a hint of how the Chase was affected by the Black Death. A William Trumwyne died that year, when the Black Death hit the Midlands and, although there is no indication of how he died, there is a fair chance that it was one type of plague or the other. It is impossible to say how many people died locally, but modern estimates suggest anything between a third and a half of the population perished. The only piece of evidence that directly refers to the effects of the Black Death is an entry in the Great Register of Lichfield. The entry records the death of John de Loges of Great Wyrleye, in 1349. It refers to his land and says, 'it used to be worth before these times 100s. and now they are worth

17 An aerial view of Wootton's timber yard, near the old *Hollies* site, Cannock, late 1950s. The pattern of fields beyond the yard was typical of how the small farms in the area had been for hundreds of years.

60s. … because of the present pestilence and the paucity of tenants.'

The Chase was part of the Cuttlestone hundred, one of the five 'hundreds' of Staffordshire. A hundred was a main subdivision of an English shire long before the Conquest. By late Anglo-Saxon times it was a judicial, fiscal and military unit of administration, and in the Middle Ages its role was mainly judicial. Each hundred had a court which met about once every three weeks, usually to deal with petty civil matters. Twice a year each court was attended by the county's sheriff, who regulated the frankpledge system and dealt with criminal matters. An Act of Parliament in 1807 finally ended the existence of the hundreds; in many areas this was a mere formality as they had long been in decline.

Frankpledge was a clever idea. Before the days of a modern police force frankpledge aimed to ensure good order in each community. Every male was expected to join a 'tithing', a group of ten men who shared collective responsibility for each others' good conduct. Failure to comply resulted in a fine or some other penalty. Frankpledge began in Saxon times but was refined by the Normans, perhaps to try to give some protection to isolated Normans in hostile areas. Hence the sheriff's twice yearly visit to ensure all who should had joined a tithing. He never went home empty-handed because he collected fines and other dues at the same time.

Frankpledge also provided individual lords of the manor with an income as they oversaw the tithings within their area of jurisdiction. From around 1309 the leet courts of Cannock and Rugeley were held jointly, usually on an alternate basis; and a twice-yearly review of frankpledge was held in the leet court as early as 1274, when Cannock was represented by five frankpledges, as was Rugeley and Brereton. By 1341 Great Wyrley was sending two frankpledges to the leet court of Cannock and paid one shilling frithsilver to the lord of the manor. In the same year Huntington also sent two frankpledge representatives. Huntington paid 6d. in frithsilver. In 1529 a shift in settlement patterns meant Cannock had been reduced to three representatives, with one representative each for Leacroft, Hednesford and Hatherton.

Although William took possession of Algar's earldom, succeeding bishops of Lichfield and Chester also had extensive land holdings locally, some of which had been held by the Church before the Conquest, other lands were acquired afterwards. In 1086 the Bishop of Lichfield and Chester held four carucates of land in Wyrley and Norton, land that was attached to the manor of Lichfield. When Ranulph, Earl of Chester, died in 1153 he granted the 'vill' of Cannock to the Cistercian abbey at Radmore, founded in 1141. This grant was sanctioned by Henry II the following year. Other endowments followed. Henry II gave land at 'Hedeneford' as pasture to the abbey. Meanwhile William Croc of Wyrley signed over rights to his lands to the abbey when he became a monk there in 1150.

We can only guess at the subsequent history of Cannock Chase had the abbey flourished like other great Cistercian communities. Unfortunately, within 15 years the monks had had enough and they left Radmore to join the main house at Stoneleigh, Warwickshire in 1155. To be fair, the community was founded during the civil upheavals caused by the struggle for power between Stephen and Matilda, and those years must have been difficult and dangerous. A year after Matilda's son, Henry II, succeeded to the throne, in 1154, he visited the area and stayed at the house at Radmore. No doubt he hunted in the royal forest, as well as consolidating his hold in the Midlands.

During Henry II's reign the manor of Cannock reverted, briefly, to the crown. Then, in 1189, Richard I, short of money for his crusade, conveyed the manors of Cannock and Rugeley to the see of Lichfield and Coventry (instead of Chester, where it had been). Shortly afterwards the bishop made the mistake of siding with John during Richard's absence. He was fined 2,000 marks for his sins; but he held on to the manors and they remained with the see of Lichfield until the dissolution of the monasteries.

The royal forest of Cannock also had a chequered history at this time. Church and Crown disputed respective rights on and off for over two centuries until 1290, when the crown formally recognised part of it as the bishop of Lichfield's 'Chase'. A 'chase' was a forest controlled by an individual rather than the monarch. In the countryside there was a vital distinction between the land protected under forest law and the land outside these laws. For centuries before there had been a gradual encroachment into waste and forest, as the population increased and more land was cultivated. There are many examples of men being fined for cutting down trees. One William del Hethe, of Great Wyrley, was sued by Thomas Hextale, for 'breaking into his close at Great Wyrley and carrying away his trees to the value of 60 shillings'. By the 12th century English forests, although still large, were merely relics of the primeval woods that had once covered the land. But what remained was guarded jealously.

Forest law in no way superseded the ordinary law of the land; rather it supplemented it. William Croc (son of William, the Radmore monk) of Great Wyrley was fined for a forest offence in 1170 and subsequently hanged. These harsh laws were rigorously enforced in the early Norman period. As a result, all sorts of anomalies developed, which often aimed to avoid imposing the severest penalties – and they could be severe! In 1198 Richard I declared those found guilty of killing deer should lose their eyes and testicles. These laws were bitterly resented and fuelled many grievances against the crown. This led Henry III to issue the 'Forest Charter' of 1217, two years after Magna Carta, which attempted to regulate forest laws and end

18 St Luke's Church, Cannock. There was a chapel at Cannock in the 12th century which was recognised as a church by 1293. It has been rebuilt and extended several times during its history. The graveyard, pictured here, is probably as old as the church itself – despite attempts lasting well into the 14th century to prevent burials at Cannock, made by officials of St Michael's, Penkridge.

the grievances felt by many. One thing the charter stated was, 'in future no-one shall lose life or limb for our venison'. Heavy fines were levied instead, and if the felon could not pay the fine then he went to prison for a year and a day.

Back in the 13th century there were still a few wolves about – although they were rare as killing a wolf carried a reward. The beasts protected by forest law were the red, fallow and roe deer, and boar, although wild boar were also scarce by the mid-13th century. During the reign of Edward III roe deer lost their protection 'because they drove away the other deer'. Not surprisingly, there was a common dislike of the forest official. One contemporary stated, 'I'd rather go to my plough than serve in such an office as yours.' One of the last forest laws to be enacted occurred in 1390 when a statute was passed which effectively forbade the poor from hunting anywhere. It marks the beginning of the notion of 'gentleman's game', whereby the landowner had sole hunting rights.

Several local families were Keepers of the King's Forest in medieval times. One Richard le Venur, or Richard the Forester, was the man in charge at the time of the Conquest. Although he was a Saxon he was permitted to retain the post, probably because of his local knowledge. His hereditary entitlement passed to his daughter's husband, William Croc. With the execution of a later William Croc the position was given to Robert de Brok, along with William's sister, Margery. Margery's opinions on her marriage to Robert haven't survived! Their daughter, another Margery, inherited the lands and forestership which immediately passed to her husband, Hugh de Loges. The male line of the de Loges ended in 1349, and with it the family's stewardship of the forest. By the 15th century the Swynnerton family were the stewards of the Forest of Cannock. The separate 'free' chase of the bishops of Lichfield had its own keepers. The de Aston family of Haywood and Bishton held the hereditary entitlement, which descended in this family, with only a couple of brief breaks, until 1538. Disputes began when the Pagets acquired the Beaudesert estate. The dispute rumbled on until 1712 when the Astons agreed to take four bucks (deer, not cash) a year and, in return, waived all other rights.

Another result of the dominance of the Church in the area was the fact that there was no resident lord in Cannock. No manor house existed in the Middle Ages; the biggest building was probably the 'lord's mill', in existence from at least 1274, which provided a service (at a price) to the local tenants. It remained in the hands of tenants for several centuries. Great Wyrley also had a mill in 1153 and it was in the hands of one Ralph the miller in 1283. A few years before, in 1259, Henry III granted the bishop of Lichfield the right to hold a weekly market at Cannock on Tuesdays, and an annual three-day fair in the middle of October.

There was a chapel at Cannock by the 12th century and, judging by a series of disputes, it may well have been a dependency of Penkridge Collegiate Church, rather than part of the see of Lichfield, as it is today. During part of this time the unsatisfactory compromise meant that the see of Lichfield held certain rights, such as appointing the chaplain, but that all parishioners of Cannock had to be buried at Penkridge and pay for the privilege! In 1330 the Dean and Chapter of Lichfield had the bishop of St Asaph secretly consecrate a graveyard at Cannock and they began to conduct their own burials and collect their own fees. By 1345 Penkridge must have decided to call it a day as there are no further records of the dispute. Of course, the Black Death may well have – quite literally – wiped it from the minds of the clergy concerned.

The population continued to decline after the first bout of the Black Death and there were further outbreaks in the years following – 1361 was particularly bad. The disease had major economic effects which only became apparent in the 1370s. A lot of arable land was given over to pasture, and labour became more expensive. Try as they might lords of the manors could not re-impose peasant labour services on the same scale as before. The introduction of the hated poll taxes to pay for the Hundred Years War with France erupted into open revolt in 1381. However, the good folk of the Chase had the sense to keep out of it.

No sooner had the Peasants Revolt subsided than the upheavals of the 15th century began to loom. The worst period was between 1455-87, which historians now class as the period of the Wars of the Roses, rather than the much longer period of unrest which spanned most of the 15th century. Although there were no major battles in the area, surviving records suggest that anarchy was rife here, on the Chase, as it was elsewhere. The forces of law and order had never been at such a low ebb. No wonder there was such jubilation when King Henry VIII succeeded to the throne in 1509.

Four
Family Fortunes

Although the Chase, like most of Staffordshire, was remote and isolated, its industrial future was starting to evolve by the end of the 15th century. The rich coalfields of South Staffordshire and East Shropshire were beginning to support a diverse range of metal industries, and even the Chase, remote as it was, began to benefit. Individuals with the skill and initiative to make the best of new opportunities were working on the Chase despite – or perhaps because of – the troubled times of the Wars of the Roses. A smith named William Colmore rented a forge near Hednesford, in 1473, for 2d. a year from the lord of Cannock. Seventy years later, in the 1540s, another local man, William Fletcher, operated 'Blome smithes' at Risom Bridge, near Beaudesert Park, which he leased from William Lord Paget.

19 Sir William Paget, an able lawyer and statesman who served King Henry VIII and his children, Edward and Mary, in turn. He rose from humble origins (one source suggested he was a son of a Wednesbury nailer) to become a knight in 1544. Paget re-established his connections with the Midlands when he acquired the estate of Beaudesert, from the Bishop of Coventry and Lichfield, in 1546.

Unlikely as it may seem, it was the Chase, and not South Staffordshire, which had the first blast furnace in the Midlands. It was built near Hednesford for William Lord Paget in 1561. The 'Risom' or Rising Brook provided the water power required, which was supplemented by three pools – the Furnace Pool and the two Brindley Pools, each lying in the valley of the Rising Brook. Despite the difficulties and the expense of transporting heavy goods, it was clearly worth Lord Paget's while to bring in good quality ironstone, low in sulphur and phosphorus, from open-cast mines in Walsall. The 'blast' was provided by two great leather bellows which were driven by a water wheel. Blast furnaces required less water power than forges which explains why the industry was not integrated at this time. The brittle pig iron had to be transported to forges built alongside more powerful water wheels.

The furnace, and a second one built near Teddesley in 1578, produced two types of pig iron. 'Tough Pig' was used to make best quality malleable bar iron, whilst 'cold-short' pig was used to make bar iron suitable for nail-making. The pig

20 An impression by John Moreton of the original layout and construction of the Cannock charcoal blast furnace of 1561. This was the first blast furnace to be built in the Midlands. It was situated on the Rising Brook, near Hednesford.

iron went to forges at Fair Oak, near Rugeley, or to Abbots Bromley. It was turned into malleable bar iron and then slit into rods that were purchased by manufacturers in South Staffordshire and Birmingham. In 1584 Paget's two furnaces produced 164 tons 1 cwt of iron; no wonder that the Chase was rapidly turning from forest to heathland with the insatiable demand for charcoal.

It must have been very frustrating for those involved to know that they were sitting on what then seemed like unlimited supplies of unusable coal as charcoal supplies rapidly diminished. Many enterprising men tried to solve the problem of how to smelt iron using 'raw pit coal', but unfortunately, although numerous patents were taken out, few written records survive. Dud Dudley's claims to success are well known, outlined in his book *Metallum Martis*, but they will probably always remain a matter of debate. If he was successful, his secret died with him in 1684. It was left to Abraham Darby, born near Dudley, to develop a profitable method of smelting iron using coke some 25 years later.

At one end of the social scale, men such as Colmore and Fletcher were helping to lay the foundations of England's transition to a capitalist society. And at the other end the great entrepreneurs of the 16th century, such as William Lord

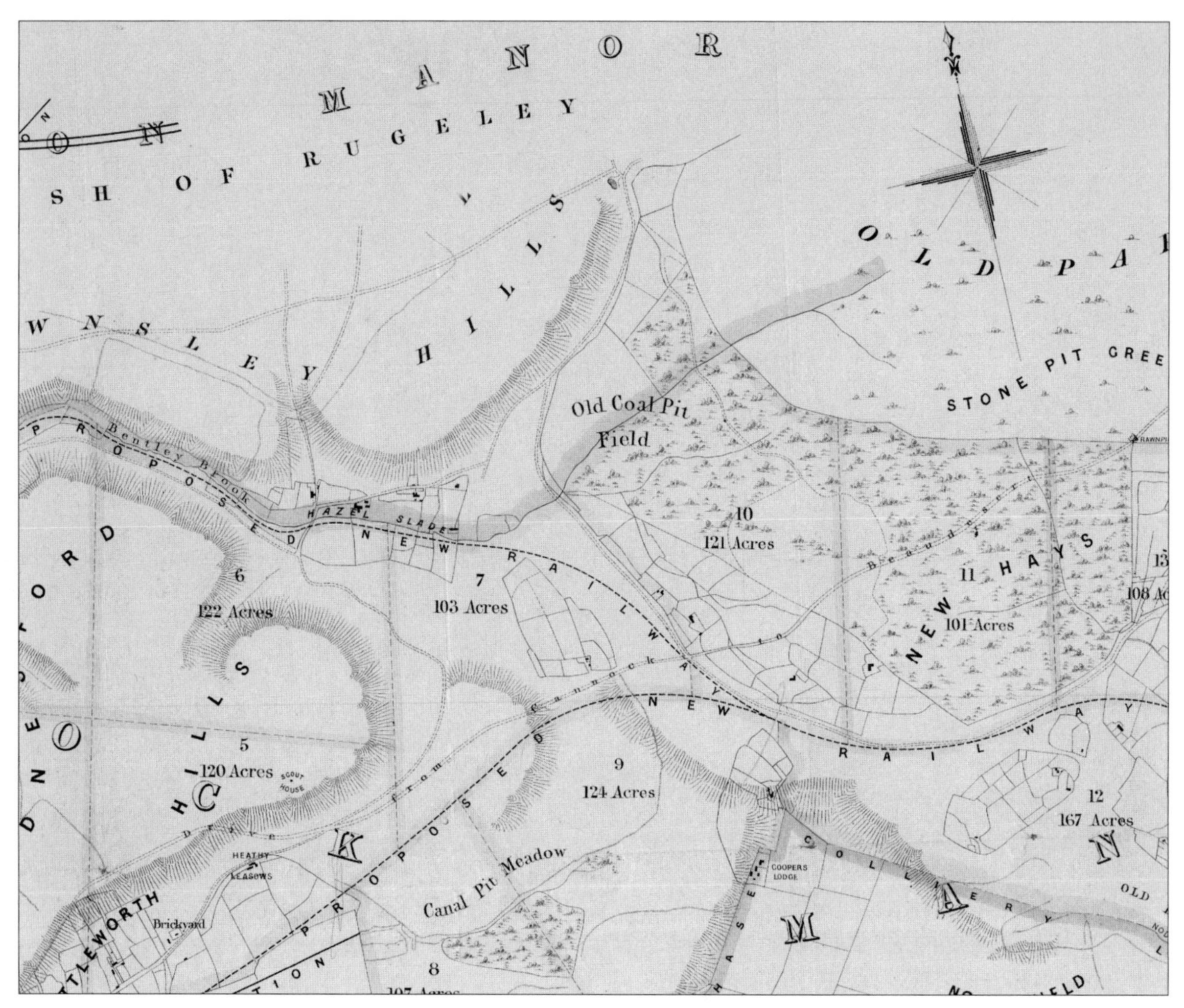

21 Old Coal Pit Field, near Beaudesert. The Coal Pit Field was situated on an outcrop of coal which had been mined for several centuries and the remains of old bell pits can still be traced in and around Beaudesert today.

Paget, began to create the conditions for the blossoming of England into a world power. William, 1st Lord Paget of Beaudesert, was a remarkable man. Rising from humble origins, he made a career first as a lawyer and then as a government minister during troubled times, the later years of Henry VIII, and then his children, Edward and Mary, in turn. Above all, he was a skilled diplomat who managed to keep his head during Henry's declining years and engineer Somerset's rise to power as Lord Protector to Edward VI. Unfortunately, Paget's clear vision and wise advice was all too often ignored by Somerset. Paget, alarmed by the near collapse of strong central government by the end of Edward's brief reign urged Mary to marry Philip of Spain. In Paget's mind Phillip offered the best hope of sound government. It was advice which Paget must have regretted many times. The result was that when Elizabeth came to the throne Paget was beyond the pale; his political career was finished. And yet, with his pragmatic, moderate views he would probably have made an excellent Elizabethan minister.

Paget was one of many self-made Englishmen of the 16th century. However, although there

22 A rare view of the rear of Beaudesert Hall, shortly before its demolition. A serious fire occurred in 1909 and the 6th Marquis spent a large amount of money on the restoration of the hall and grounds. Sadly, it was not enough to save Beaudesert. The First World War was the death knell of many an aristocratic estate. Between 1919 and 1935 the estate, the hall and its contents were sold.

has always been room for people to rise to the top of English society, snobbery still prevailed. Because of this Paget did his best to keep his origins obscure. Modern research strongly suggests that his father was John Pachet of London, described by Paget's biographer as a 'jack-of-all-trades' and a sergeant of London. One contemporary source stated that Paget's father was born in Wednesbury but there is stronger evidence to suggest that John Pachet was related to a Worcestershire family. It is known that William's father made several loans to Worcestershire people whilst he lived in London. William attended St Paul's School and was educated alongside other future government ministers such as Thomas Wriothesley, later the Earl of Southampton. He went on to Cambridge University where his potential was recognised. He then studied at the

23 Part of the gardens of Beaudesert Hall, which must have been a beautiful sight in years gone by. In 1798, Stebbing Shaw, in his *The History and Antiquities of Staffordshire*, said, 'The walks and pleasure grounds, on every side of the house, are particularly well laid out with the simplicity that forms true grandeur …'.

University of Paris. His career as a leading diplomat was cast.

In January 1544 Paget became Sir William Paget, knight. At this time he was granted the manors of Bromley in Staffordshire and Edleston in Derbyshire. Other honours soon followed. However, the most profitable was Beaudesert. In October 1546 the bishop of Coventry and Lichfield was forced to surrender to the king six manors in Staffordshire, including the mansion and manor of Beaudesert. Paget paid a huge sum – £2,708 to Henry and a further £3,000 to the Court of Augmentations – for Beaudesert and its six manors, as well as lands in Burton. Paget paid his debt in five annual instalments. Paget knew his lands represented wealth and power but little did he realise that the coal that lay under Beaudesert promised even greater wealth in the future.

Paget was ahead of his time in various ways: promoting new technology on his Staffordshire estates and urging against England's isolationist policies in Europe. He was also offering advice on how to deal with the debased coinage that was causing such inflation and misery to poorer folk. He died in June 1563 and his body was buried at West Drayton in Middlesex. Later his son, Thomas, erected a fine monument in his memory at Lichfield Cathedral only for it to be destroyed by Puritan vandals during the Civil War in the next century.

The 16th century was a remarkable one in many ways. Opportunities abounded for the enterprising and adventurous but fear and persecution menaced many more. How many Chase folk witnessed the burning of the three Lichfield martyrs during Mary's reign? Undoubtedly the majority bent to whichever doctrinal wind was blowing at the time; perhaps people were taking their lead from William Paget's pragmatic approach. In 1604 the 400 people of Cannock were labelled as 'almost all papists'. The Coleman family were Roman Catholics who were prepared to be counted. Walter Coleman was listed as a recusant in 1607 and his son, John, is listed as a recusant in 1641. Finally, in 1667, Charles Coleman was convicted as a recusant. At least they did not die for their beliefs!

The Reformation brought some changes to St Luke's, Cannock, although records are scarce. The church was not well endowed. A chantry dedicated to Our Lady , founded in 1421, possessed lands, including Mokynton Place at Hednesford, tithes, ten cows and £1 6s. 8d. for the support of a chantry priest. The same priest also ran a grammar school for parishioners' children between 1518 and 1548, the year the chantry was dissolved. The priest, Laurence Peryn, was ordered to continue teaching for a salary of £4 14s. 5½d. a year. The chantry lands were sold to John Cupper and Richard Trevour in 1549. By 1552 William Paget had acquired them and the lands and tithes became part of the manor of Cannock until at least 1788, by which time later generations of the Paget family were poised to make a fortune from their mineral rights.

Five

A Skirmish at Cannock

16 Dec. 1643	For the provision beinge sente to Cannocke.	£2
(Between 16 Dec. 1643 and 27 May 1645, 33 lewns are raised 'for necessary uses' amounting to £152 5s. 0d.)		
27 Mar. 1645	For carriage of cooles for Lichfield and for provision for Lichfield.	£2
14 Nov. 1645	For provision for haye and flax and other provision.	£3
10 Mar. 1645/6	For provision.	£5
(Between 11 April and 3 Aug. 1646, 7 lewns are raised for contribution or provision 'for the towne' amounting to £40.)		
14 Aug. 1646	For the releife of those that are visited with sicknesse within Litchfeild and Stafford and other townes adjacent.	£1
12 Sept. 1646	For the disbandinge of the forces off this countye.	£20
26 Oct. 1646	For the releife of the Bretish army for Ireland, beinge the arrears of two yeares last past.	£9
22 Jan. 1646/7	For the howsse of correction and other arreares for the towne.	£2
8 June 1647	For the repaireing of bridges and money for the Kinge's Bench and for other uses within the county.	£1
2 Sept. 1647	For the quarteringe of souldiers. *(deleted)*	£12
15 Nov. 1647	For the quarteringe of souldiers.	£2
26 Nov. 1647	For the quarteringe of souldiers.	£2
17 Dec. 1647	For the quarteringe of soldiers and other necessaryes.	£2
3 Jan. 1647/8	*(Ditto.)*	£2
19 Jan. 1647/8	*(Ditto.)*	£1
24 Jan. 1647/8	*(Ditto.)*	£1
27 April 1648	For the howse of correction and gaole money and for Mr. Babington, and for other necessary uses for the towne.	£1
16 Oct. 1648	For the assesment for the armye and other necessarys.	£2
16 Nov. 1648	For the quarteringe of souldiers and other necessary uses.	£6
23 Nov. 1648	*(Ditto.)*	£2
7 Feb. 1648/9	*(Ditto.)*	£4

24 Extracts from the *Lewn Book of Hatherton*. Hatherton was a small township and its inhabitants kept a careful record of all the 'lewns and assessments' which they had to pay during the war. It is recorded that they felt 'much opprest and impoverished' by the burden of supporting the war – first meeting Royalist demands and then Parliament's.

The area was divided in its loyalties during the Civil Wars, although the majority of people must have regarded the events in the country as a nightmare, best avoided if possible. James I and his son, Charles I, lacked both political acumen and the force of personality to govern the country well. It must have been a rude shock to James when he arrived in England to realise that the English Parliament actually expected to take a real part in governing the country. By the early 17th century, the concept of the Divine Right of Kings didn't really square with the modern way of doing things. The early Stuarts had neither a standing army nor a paid bureaucracy to help them rule as they wished. Their other problem was an inadequate income from legal sources, including parliamentary taxation. Charles's high-handed attempts to raise cash by other means, including the introduction of 'ship money', put him on a disastrous collision course with his subjects.

At first either side might have been victorious. The Battle of Edgehill in October 1642 was a bloody but indecisive affair. Within a month the Sheriff of Staffordshire issued a proclamation at the quarter sessions that the county was to raise a troop of 800 foot soldiers and 200 'carbynes' for the king. The three 'small' hundreds of Cuttlestone, Seisdon and Totmonslow had to provided half the numbers between them. Thomas Fowke and Thomas Whitgreave were appointed captains of the foot and Richard Congreave captain of the horse in Cuttlestone. They were responsible for training and exercising the men in readiness to fight. There seemed to be very little enthusiasm for the king and Lord Paget's attempt to raise a troop of volunteers on his behalf was a failure.

25 Thomas Tyldesley, Cannock, January 1646. Thomas Tyldesley was born in 1612 in Lancashire. He and his family were Roman Catholics. At the outbreak of the civil war, in 1642, he joined the Royalist army. The picture is a reconstruction by Christa Hook and it depicts an incident at Cannock when Tyldesley encountered Captain Stone, the Parliamentarian governor of Stafford. After fierce fighting Tyldesley managed to escape on a stray horse. He died fighting in a skirmish at Wigan, less than a month before the end of hostilities.

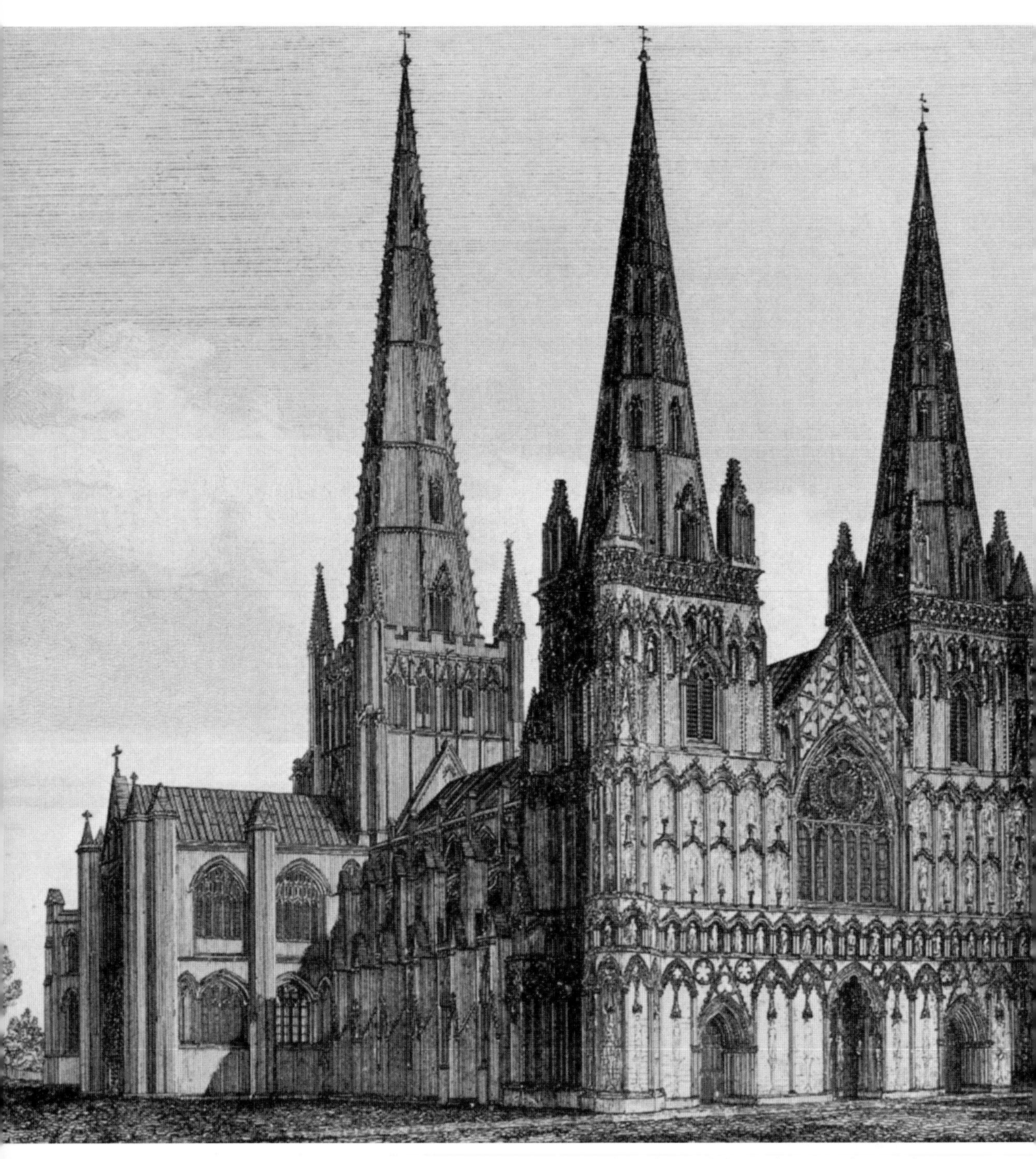

26 Lichfield Cathedral was the most badly damaged cathedral in the English Civil Wars. This was because it was still protected by a fortified medieval close. The cathedral suffered three sieges between 1643 and 1646. Miners from Cannock Chase have the distinction of being the first men to lay a landmine in England. They tunnelled under the north-west tower and blew it up with gunpowder. The picture shows the cathedral after it had been restored by Bishop Hacket.

27 Leacroft Old Farm. Leacroft was part of the ancient township of Cannock, along with Hednesford and Cannock Wood. It was probably one of the earliest farms in the district as it stood on light, well-drained soil. It was part of the estate of John Byrche during his lifetime. It must have been a profitable part, as his Leacroft rents yielded £100 a year before the wars.

The following year the war came to the west Midlands. The Battle of Hopton Heath, near Stafford, took place on 19 March 1643. It led to the Parliamentarians taking control of Stafford for the rest of the war. In the same month, at the first siege of Lichfield, the Royalists briefly lost control of the fortified cathedral close. Around the same time, Henrietta Maria, wife of Charles I, arrived from Holland after trying to raise money by selling the crown jewels. She brought arms and ammunition with her and Prince Rupert had the task of clearing a safe route from Bridlington, in the north east, to Oxford, where one of the king's armies was based. It was a tall order as there were many parliamentary garrisons to deal with en route. Arriving in Birmingham on 3 April, Rupert encountered fierce opposition, especially from the citizens of Deritend. In the skirmish that became known as the 'Birmingham Butcheries' the Royalist earl of Denbigh was gravely injured and he died five days later at Cannock. His son, who succeeded him, sided with Parliament; one of many examples of divided family loyalties during the wars.

The Birmingham incident did not reflect well on Prince Rupert, who was angrily rebuked by Charles. Possibly because of this he was much more cautious when he took Rushall Hall near Walsall, which was stoutly defended by the wife of Colonel Leigh. What must the people of Cannock have thought when they heard the news? Rushall was only a few miles away, but a strategic point on the route between Manchester, Coventry and London. It remained in Royalist hands

Ranton Abby
Seighford
Cresswell
Hopton heath
Stafford
Tixall heath
Ranton
Aston
Doxy
Knightley
Clanford gr
Derrington
S: Thomas
Knightley Park
Brasnill
Stallbrook
Staff: Cast
Rowley
Broughhall
Moore end
Hollies
Haughton
Billington
Butterton
Hyde
Baswich
Weeping Cross
Allmoore
Gnosall
Burton
O: Rewl
Darnsdale
Ricarscot
Coton
Copenall
Penk flu:
N: Rewl
Bednall
Cowley
Alston
Apeton
Barton
Dunston
Acton Trussell
Wood Eyton
Bradeley
Teddesley head
Church Eyton
Shredicot
Levedale
High-On
Drayton
Wollaston
Preston
Orslow
Little On
Mitton
Wolgaston
G: Chatwall
Marston
Penkridg
Whiston
Bitham
Brineton
Longnor
Congreve
Otherton
Bickford
Blym hill
Pillaton
High hall
Lapley
Hatherton
Ivetsey
Wheaten Aston
Kinnerston
Rodbaston
Stretton
Cannock
Water Eaton
Fower crosses
Horsebrook
Engleton
G: Sarden
Cheslin hay
Brewood
Somerford
Blackladies
Kidimoor green
L Sarden
Bishops wood
Hyde
Forgehouses
Crakeford
Shareshall
Boscobell
Coven
Chillington
Landy
Royall Oake
Asspley
Longburch
Hatton
Fetherston
Hilton
Codsall wood
Gunston
Brinsford
Moseley
Codsall
Penford
Oaken
Ford houses
Bilbrook
Kingswood
Bushbury
Barnhurst
Oxley
Old fallings

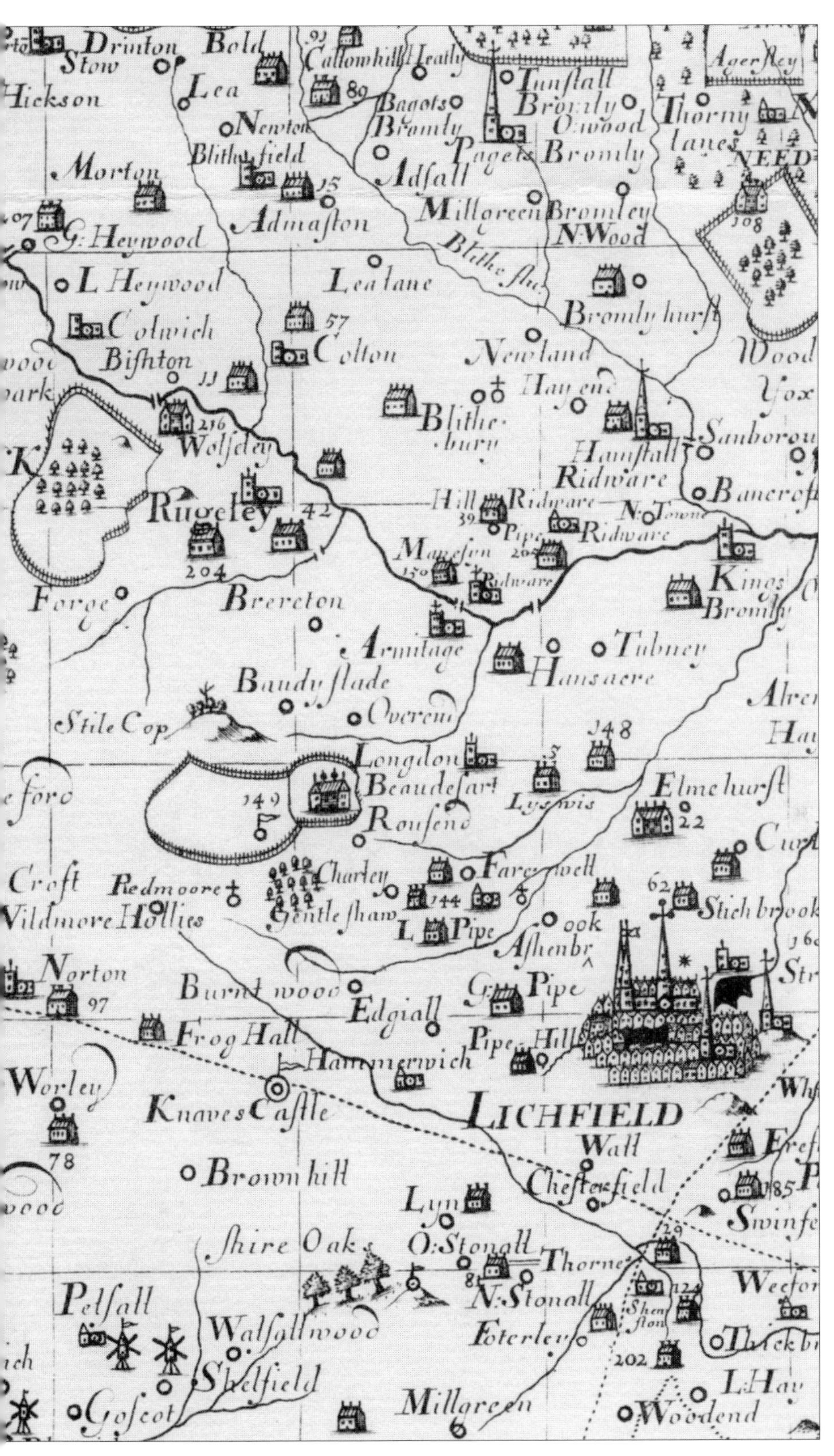

28 Part of a map from Robert Plot's *The Natural History of Staffordshire.* There are some fascinating variations in the spellings of local place names such as *Fower crosses* and *Cheslin hay.* The numbers next to the places such as Beaudesert relate to the coats of arms of all the leading families of Staffordshire (shown around the edge of the map). 149, for example, refers to the Paget coat of arms.

for some time. Rupert passed through Cannock, where the earl of Denbigh died, and then made for Lichfield, arriving there on 7 April.

Again fighting was dangerously close to the Chase. When the Parliamentarians had taken Lichfield in early March 1643, its Royalist defenders had had their moment of triumph when a Mr. Dyott shot and killed Lord Brooke, the leader of the besieging Parliamentary troops. Dyott used a primitive, unwieldy and very long duck gun, taking aim from one of the spires of the cathedral. He hit his target over a remarkably long distance. It was such an unlikely shot that the Royalists saw it as a sign that God was on their side. Only three days later, however, they were forced to surrender.

Rupert arrived with around seven thousand troops. He demanded the surrender of the garrison but Colonel Russell, the leader, refused. The events at Deritend had marred Rupert's reputation; could he be trusted? Rupert retaliated by bombarding the north wall and the South Gate of the Cathedral Close. This failed. He then ordered some fifty miners from Cannock Chase to tunnel under the north walls of the Close, to undermine them with the aid of gunpowder. The north-west corner tower was breached on 20 April, the first time a landmine was used in Britain. After fierce fighting the Parliamentarians surrendered to Rupert the following day. Lichfield Cathedral then remained in Royalist hands until July 1646.

The wars brought many strangers into the area. Thomas Tyldesley, a Royalist soldier born in Lancashire, was one. He had spent some years in Europe as a soldier before returning home, in 1634, to marry. As a Catholic it was natural that he joined the king's forces once the appeal went out. He fought in Manchester in July 1642 and at Edgehill on 22 October 1642. He survived an attack at Preston and an ambush at Pendle. In the spring of 1643 he joined the Queen's escort, which safely delivered ammunition to Oxford. A little later Tyldesley was knighted after fighting at Burton-on-Trent. His luck ran out when he was captured, and he was imprisoned at Eccleshall and then Stafford Castle, but he escaped late in 1645. He became governor of the Royalist garrison at Lichfield Cathedral and led the defence of the Close in the third siege, which ended in surrender – on the direct orders of the king – in July 1646. Tyldesley supported the king, and then his son, until his death during fighting at Wigan in August 1651.

He sounds like a character from an Errol Flynn or Kevin Costner film, and his narrow escape in a skirmish at Cannock, in January 1646, is typical. After his escape from Stafford Castle, he was given command of the Royalist horse in Staffordshire. On 9 January 1646 Tyldesley and three troops of horse encountered Captain Stone, the Parliamentarian governor of Stafford, near Cannock – possibly on Calving Hill. At first the Royalists seemed to be winning but Tyldesley's horse fell and unseated him. Undeterred, and with some of Captain Stone's men in hot pursuit, he ran through a nearby house and escaped on a stray horse. His cloak, hat and own horse were carried off to Stafford as war trophies by Stone's men.

John Byrche of Cannock did not have a very good war. He joined Sir William Whitmore's garrison at Bridgnorth but was apprehended in January 1643 and arrested for high treason. Byrche was kept in Shrewsbury gaol for a year, then exchanged for Colonel Sneyd, a Parliamentarian, by the Committee at Stafford. The Committee was very put out when Byrche rejoined Sir William at Bridgnorth, rather than go straight to Stafford to make amends. He spent six months at Sir William Whitmore's before the garrison fell to the Parliamentary troops. He also made matters worse when he 'lent tenne pounds, as we are credibly informed, to the King's Commissioners'. The committee estimated that Byrche's estates in Cannock and Warwickshire were worth £280 per annum. Details of his estate survive: apparently, before the wars Leacroft rents yielded £100 annually, nearby Kingswood £60, land in Cannock £50, and his wife's life interest in lands at Sutton Coldfield and Drayton Bassett another £72. In June 1645 Byrche petitioned the Committee at Stafford for some of his income to be returned. Byrche had a wife and five children to support and he had debts of more than £800. But how did he feel when he promised the Committee in future to 'doe any service in the cause you have in hand'? The entry ends with a rather telling note: 'He (Byrche) in his absence hath sent intelligence to Stafford of the enimye's intentions.'

The unpaid parish officers also had a difficult time during these years. They had the unenviable task of collecting money for the Committee at Stafford. A complaint about some inhabitants of Great Wyrley who were not pulling their weight illustrates this point. One official wrote, ' ... yet many contentious persons reside amongst us ... refuse and neglecte to doe and performe ther equall portion wherby the generall of us are much wronged ... '. The expense of the wars was crippling and another source of resentment. Fourteen inhabitants of Hatherton township wrote to the local JPs requesting a reassessment of the township's tax burden, which they all stated was very unfair. They claimed that they were 'much opprest and impoverished by reason of the inequalitie of our lewns and assessments'. A remarkable range of payments were recorded in the Hatherton Lewn Book. Six pounds was spent on equipping a 'souldier' between April 1639 and June 1640. This anonymous soldier probably marched north, from Uttoxeter, with the king's army to fight the Scots in the Bishops' Wars. Apparently, whilst at Uttoxeter, quite a few men from Seisdon and Cuttlestone hundreds burnt their way out of the fenced enclosure in which they were camped, and tried to escape. There were nine men at Uttoxeter from Cannock, Huntington and Great Wyrley; one, Thomas Burrowes, managed to go sick and another, Robert White, fled. Going to Scotland to fight about the finer points of religious doctrine must have seemed pretty barmy, even in those days.

There are two costly entries made in 1643 'for the prevention of plunderinge and pilligine of his Majestie's subjects – £5'. In October 1646 another £9 was sent 'for the releife of the Bretish army for Ireland, beinge the arrears of two years last past'. Later there is evidence of the effects of war – 29 March 1653, £1 'for the necessary repayre of the parrish church of Wolverhampton ... and for the maymed souldiers'. Another payment of £2 for the church and 'maymed souldiers' was made in February 1657. And in 1659 there is an entry which must have gladdened the hearts of every sensible person – 30 September, 'Towards the disbanding of the new rayesd forces in this country. – £7 10s. 0d.'. King Charles II arrived back in England the following year.

Six

The Beginning of the End

The earliest photographs of Cannock town centre show a wide market square flanked by the ancient bowling green, shops and homes, the old *Crown Hotel* and St Luke's. Mature lime trees around the church and bowling green add to the charm of the place. At High Green, lying alongside the road to Penkridge, stood a lovely Georgian house named 'The Green', which still exists today. The old manor house stood virtually opposite. Only the new Market Hall, built in 1869, hinted at progress. Altogether the town gave the impression of a pleasant, well-ordered rural community, quite content, in no hurry, and pretty satisfied with itself.

The alarms and excursions of the 17th century were just a distant memory. Throughout the 18th century the country seemed to be on an upward

29 A view of part of Cannock which was much the same at the end of the 18th century. Curiously, although the house known as 'The Green' existed then, it was not until the mid-19th century that its owner, Bernard Gilpin, gave it a 'Georgian' façade.

curve. Prosperity for many, and the new consumerism that went with it, pointed to a brighter future. Enlightenment and confidence in all things British underpinned respectable society. That is not to say passions did not run high over important issues of the day. Religious matters, in particular, upset the Chase's tranquillity (along with the rest of the country) on more than one occasion. Cannock found itself in the limelight in 1709 when the curate of St Luke's, Henry Sacheverell, a fiery political preacher, roundly attacked the Whig government.

Born in Marlborough in 1674, and educated at Oxford, Henry gained his doctorate in 1708. He was a High Church Tory supporter who firmly believed that the established Anglican Church was under threat from Dissenters, and that the government was doing nothing about the risk. Sacheverell delivered his first contentious sermon at Derby assizes and the second at St Paul's, London. He was impeached before the House of Lords the following year. Rioters destroyed meeting houses in London to show their support for Sacheverell, much to the alarm of Queen Anne and her government. It was probably this sense that things could easily escalate which tempered his punishment. Consequently, Sacheverell was dealt with lightly; he was merely forbidden to preach for three years. It did him no harm. In 1713, a new Tory government invited him to deliver the Restoration sermon to the House of Commons. Sacheverell was also given a much richer parish than Cannock, that of St Andrew's, Holborn. He remained a Jacobite supporter for the rest of his life. He sounds as though he was a difficult person to get on with, to say the least. It is said that Sacheverell often fell out with his new parishioners in Holborn. He died in 1724.

Religious bigotry of a different sort also raised its ugly head in the late 1820s. This time Roman Catholics bore the brunt of popular prejudice. Catholic Emancipation was long overdue but it took the very real threat of civil war in Ireland to force the Bill (granting more, rather than equal, rights) through Parliament in 1829. The unlikely combination of two staunch Protestants, the Prime Minister, the Duke of Wellington, and Sir Robert Peel, ensured the success of the Act, but they paid a heavy price. Their actions brought about the demise of the old Tory party, which was voted out of office the following year.

30 The United Reformed Chapel, Cannock. Erected in 1824, it was originally known as the Independent Chapel, and later the Congregational Church. The manse still stands next door but it is now swallowed up by the college site.

The 'undersigned householders and inhabitants of Cannock' made their feelings known in a petition to the House of Lords at the height of the crisis. The petition was just one of many similar pleas from across the country. Cannock's petitioners argued that granting Papists the right to become MPs or hold high executive office would be a dangerous threat to the Protestant Constitution and they urged 'the Lords Spiritual and Temporal' to have nothing to do with the Bill. Luckily, wiser council prevailed, war was averted, and within a few years people must have been wondering what all the fuss was about.

In between the Sacheverell and Catholic Emancipation episodes, Methodism had begun to make

31 Linford's shop, Cannock. The firm of Charles Linford was founded in 1877. The building, now a public house, is one of the oldest in Cannock.

its mark in the area. John Wesley visited the Midlands many times. In February 1746 he struggled along Blake Street, between Brownhills and Stafford, during a terrible snowstorm. It is known that he preached at Great Wyrley and Hednesford during his ministry. His attacks on the lax example of the established church struck a chord with many ordinary people. The idea that it was possible to improve one's lot in life through hard work, education and respectability had a wide appeal. In the early days Methodists worshipped outdoors or in private homes. Gradually, money was found to build places of worship. The first local Methodist Chapel was built at Cheslyn Hay some time between 1816 and 1819. This, in turn, was replaced by the Salem Church, erected in 1861, to meet the needs of the growing congregation. Many more chapels were built across the district, often to accommodate the Methodist miners and their families from the Black Country, Wales and Shropshire. Other non-conformist places of worship were built as well. In 1824 Cannock's Congregational Church was erected. It is still there, on the corner of Park Road, a little bit of Cannock's past hemmed in by modern developments.

During the 19th century, paternalism, humanitarianism and religious fervour led to all sorts of generous public endowments for the betterment of society. The Chase saw its fair share of such activity. Mrs. Moreton Walhouse of Hatherton Hall, for example, paid for the erection of Walhouse National School in 1828. A whole host of local worthies, as well as the great and the good, endowed the National School at Great Wyrley in 1849. It was built next to St Mark's for £700. The Queen Dowager, the Duke of Sutherland, Lord Hatherton, the Gilpins, Husseys and Hanburys headed the list of subscribers. Such local family names appear time and time again, whenever an appeal for money was made. There was a real sense that wealth and status also conferred responsibilities towards the lower ranks of society.

Even those of more modest means got in on the act. In 1860, Mr. Sydenham, Head Master of Cannock Grammar School, found the 'buildings in a miserable condition, with no funds to improve them' so he offered the school's trustees the profits from 1,000 copies of a history book which he intended to write. They accepted his offer and within four months 880 copies had been sold by private subscription. Supporters received public recognition when their names were listed at the front of the book. Many were local people, but there are some curious addresses; two gentlemen called Bickford, for example, lived in Paradise!

The town enjoyed the reputation of being a healthy place and people even came to drink the local water. In 1854 the town's supply was deemed to be as good as Malvern water. As early as 1735 the Byrche family of Leacroft had allowed

32 The Conduit Head, Cannock. One of the six pumps is clearly visible. Linford's hardware shop is in the background.

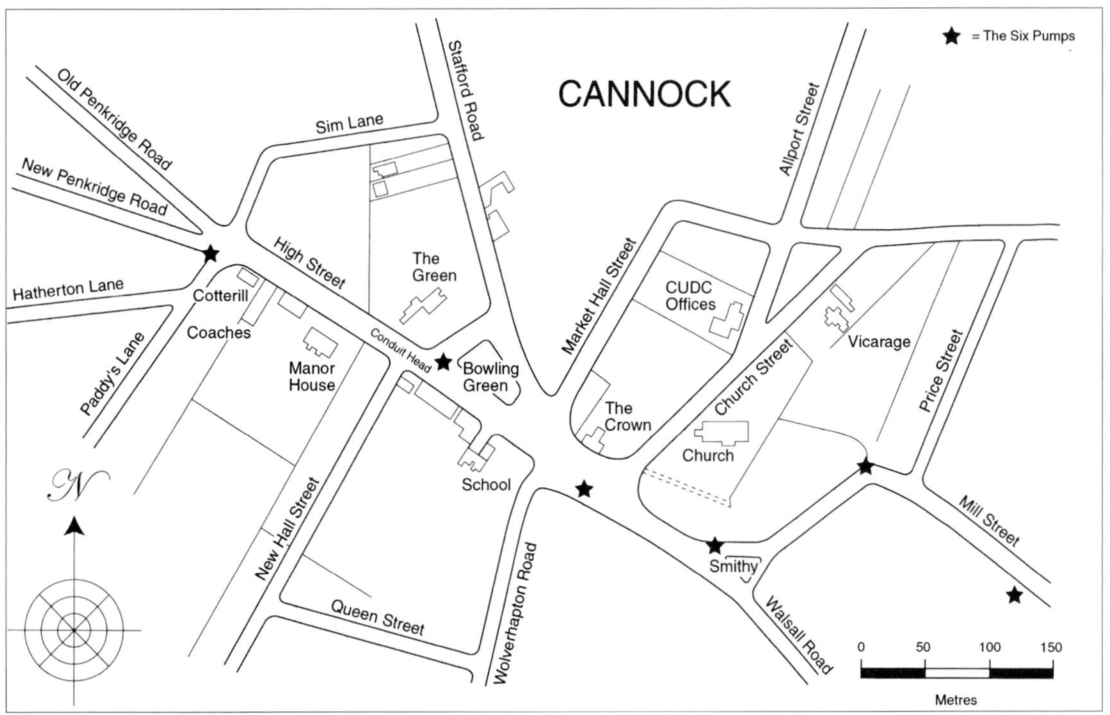

33 Location of the six pumps which were part of the Cannock Conduit Trust. As the population of Cannock grew so did the demand for fresh water. The six pumps were situated at strategic points around the town. In 1927 the pump at the corner of Mill Street and the Walsall Road was disconnected. The one at the corner of Hatherton Road and New Penkridge Road was removed in 1931 to make way for road improvements. By July 1939 the water was so contaminated that the cisterns and pumps were shut down.

34 The Manor House, Cannock. Parts of the building dated back to the 17th century. It was sold for £4,450 in 1936 and was demolished within a month of its sale. The former Danilo cinema, shops, a car park and Manor Avenue were built on its site.

35 D.W. Clarke's and the old Lloyd's Bank building, Cannock town centre. Clarke's was the nearest thing to a department store that Cannock ever had. The present Yorkshire Bank now stands on the corner of this site. Lloyd's Bank was part of an elegant Georgian house, one of several fine buildings which were demolished in the name of 'improvement', much to the detriment of the town.

spring water on their land at Rheumore Hill (now Rumer Hill) to be piped to Cannock town centre. Dr. William Byrche also donated £100 towards the costs. Initially, 49 subscribers agreed to support the project; it is interesting to note that only six could not write their name. 'The Green' was the only house permitted its own piped water; it belonged to Dr. Byrche but was rented by Sir Robert Fisher. Other inhabitants had to make do with taking water from the conduit head, which still exists today – a small hexagonal building at the far corner of the bowling green and overlooking what was, for many years, Linford's shop. Eventually there were six conduit pumps sited around the town. The records of the trust show that income was often a problem and maintenance costs turned out to be much higher than anticipated. Mining, in particular, took its toll and eventually subsidence and lack of maintenance put paid to the scheme during the Second World War. In September 1946 the agreement to take water from Newlands Well was formally concluded.

The changing occupations of the trustees over the years reflect the evolution of local society. One of the original trustees was Thomas Sant, a cordwainer in 1736. In 1783 he was the only surviving trustee, but he now styled himself 'gentleman'; he represented upwardly mobile 'Old Cannock'. Then, in 1814, one of the first local entrepreneurs of the Industrial Revolution joined the board, William Gilpin of Wedges Mills. He was a successful businessman, but he too styled himself gentleman. A further shift is evident by 1883. Of the new board of trustees only two styled themselves esquire, the rest identified themselves by their trade or profession: surgeon, draper, printer, relieving officer and collector. Here is evidence that, more and more, the middle classes were becoming actively involved in local government of one sort or another.

This trend had begun with the Reform Act of 1832, which enfranchised prosperous middle-class men. The county polling book of 1835 lists 50 voters in the parish of Cannock, including Edward Sant, grandson of Thomas, the gentleman. Further reform in 1867 and 1884 extended voting rights to most skilled workers. The right to vote was

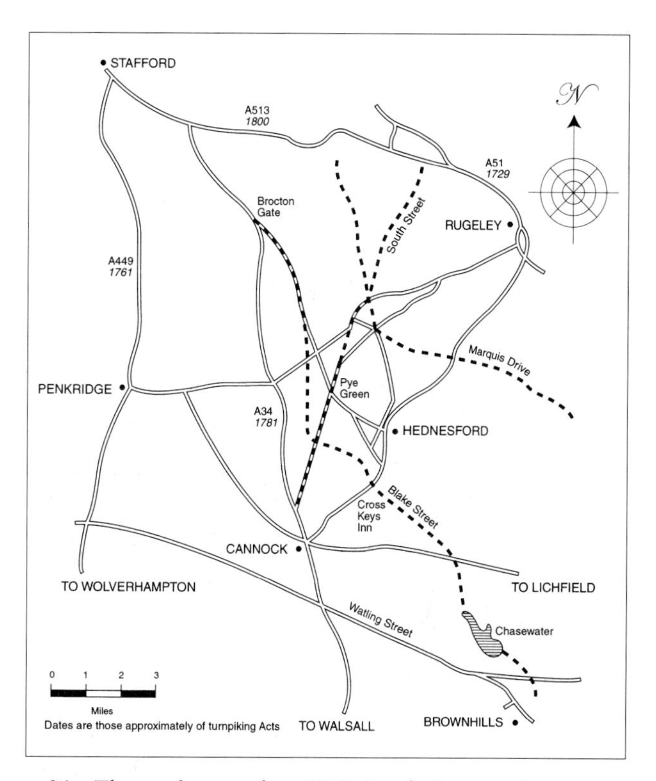

36 The road network, *c*.1800. South Street and Blake Street were ancient trackways which are probably thousands of years old. Although its origins are obscure, Blake Street may well have been a saltway to London from the Midlands and the north. It became an important coaching route until it was eclipsed by the turnpike roads of the 18th century.

not taken for granted; the enfranchised regarded civic responsibilities as a duty and a privilege. And being seen to do one's duty was, of course, a bonus. I doubt whether many would have been in favour of the recently imposed 'cabinet style' of local government, enabling far too many important decisions to be made behind closed doors.

Middle-class enterprise and vision was often behind the many improvements, changes and developments in transport. First roads, then canals and finally railways. Cannock owed its existence to the network of roads that ran through the town. Roads to and from Penkridge, Lichfield, Stafford, Rugeley and Walsall all converged on Cannock – no wonder there were so many inns. The success of Cannock's market had always depended on these roads, together with the Watling Street, which

37 The Toll House, on the Cannock to Penkridge road. An earlier painting shows the house with a barrier across the road, to ensure the collection of tolls. It is doubtful whether anyone could have foreseen the coming of the Birmingham Northern Relief Road, complete with 21st century toll booths, at the time this photograph was taken.

38 The *Four Crosses Inn*, Hatherton. The inn was kept by the Lovatt family for more than two hundred years. The inn catered for daily coach travellers and also drovers moving animals from Wales to London. The convoys of animals were kept in fields around the inn. On the green outside the inn was a big iron ring to which the animals were tied in order to shoe them. It is said that some of these convoys were a mile in length.

provided a direct, albeit slow, route to London. This old Roman road was also an important drovers' route from Shropshire and Wales. Ancient inns such as the *Fleur De Lys* near Norton Canes and *The Four Crosses* at Hatherton, both on the Watling Street, owed their existence to the steady stream of travellers in both directions.

But all these roads were tortuously slow and often very dangerous. Privately funded turnpike roads were the answer. Some of these roads were a great improvement, and very profitable; but people grumbled bitterly about having to pay. The heated debates about the rights and wrongs of the BNRR are nothing new. Back in the 1780s a well-run turnpike road on a busy route must have seemed a pretty safe investment. It remains to be seen whether the BNRR will last any longer than previous toll roads. It was left to a Walsall man, Thomas Fletcher who kept the *George Hotel*, to obtain a Turnpike Act to improve the road to Stafford, via Cannock, in 1781. The benefits were obvious, and traffic and trade greatly increased along the route. At this time local turnpike charges averaged out at 12d. per four-wheeled vehicle, 6d. per two-wheeled vehicle, 1d. per horse, ½d. per ass, large drove animals 10d. per score, and small ones, such as sheep and pigs, 5d. per score.

The age of the turnpikes marked the end of ancient routes such as Blake Street and South Street. Blake Street may well have been one of the oldest roads in the country. It is very likely that it was a salt way and a packhorse route to London. It started to cross the Chase at Knaves Castle, on the Watling Street. It passed through modern Chasewater and on just north of Five Ways, then down past the *Cross Keys* at Old Hednesford. It then proceeded along Stafford Lane, along the Huntington Belt, past Deakin's Grave and St Chad's Ditch. Blake Street then passed west of the Cank Thorn (near the original military cemetery) and joined the Stafford Road at Brocton Gate. South or Sow Street, equally ancient, joined the Chase between Wolseley Bridge and Seven Springs; it went on until it crossed Marquis Drive and then ran along the Penkridge to Rugeley Road for a short while. At Pye Green it ran in a straight line to Cannock. The new roads must have deprived Hednesford and the *Cross Keys* inn

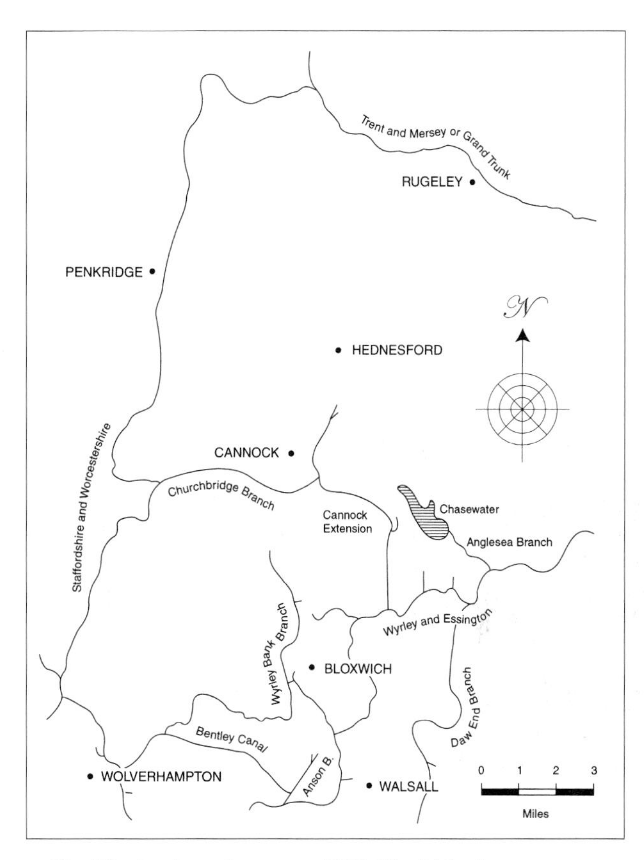

39 The local canal system, *c.*1870. The high plateau of the Chase proved to be a barrier to transport until the arrival of the railways. Despite the profits to be made from coal, no canal was ever built across the Chase. The pool at Chasewater became a vital part of the water supply of the BCN, which was often desperately short of water because of its many locks.

of much of the income from travellers, once Blake Street was bypassed. Fortunately, any loss of income from stage-coach traffic was offset by the stables round about, and Hednesford managed to maintain its reputation as a first-class training ground for racehorses.

The arrival of canals revolutionised the transport of heavy goods. The story of the construction of the Trent and Mersey Canal is well known - masterminded as it was by Josiah Wedgwood and built by James Brindley. It was opened in 1777 but as it merely skirted the northern fringes of the Chase it had little direct impact on the area, other than at Rugeley. Undeterred, Chase investors looked to the Staffs and Worcester Canal as a means of opening

40 East Cannock Canal Basin, near Hednesford. The coal-loading wharf was one of several collection points for Chase coal. Narrowboats carried the coal into the West Midlands; initially for domestic fires or steam power, and by the 1930s for coal-fired power stations.

up the Chase. The canal opened in 1772, passing by on the western rim of the Chase, but men such as Lord Hatherton saw the potential of local branches and spurs. The Hatherton Branch (also called the Churchbridge Branch), built between 1839 and 1841, was named after him. Together with the Wyrley and Essington Canal, running from the BCN at Wolverhampton, the Hatherton Branch signalled the end of the Chase's isolation.

The Wyrley and Essington Canal was authorised in 1792, at the height of 'canal mania'. It was soon moving coal from Wyrley and, within a few years, goods from William Gilpin's edge tools at Churchbridge. The relatively late development of the concealed Chase coalfield meant that some of the last canals in the country were built here, as late as the 1850s and '60s. This was quite a bold move at a time when railways had already made some canal routes unprofitable.

National rail routes through Staffordshire were constructed throughout the 1840s. Local lines into and across the Chase came in the 1850s, as the coalfield began to be developed. A branch of the South Staffordshire Railway was built from Walsall to Cannock in 1858. This joined the Cannock Mineral Line which ran from Cannock to Rugeley the following year. The Mineral Line joined the London Line at Rugeley. Other mineral lines criss-crossed the Chase, shunting coal to central collection points such as the East Cannock Canal Basin. Railways promised undreamed-of freedom to the ordinary person, from shopping trips to Walsall to day trips to the seaside. Boys were able to travel to the grammar schools at Rugeley and Walsall and their fathers could consider commuting to work.

So, in little over seventy years, the transport revolution had finally broken down the isolation of the Chase. The high central plateau was no longer a barrier to travellers. The area was about to become one of Staffordshire's key industrial areas. Cannock's days as a quiet backwater were well and truly numbered.

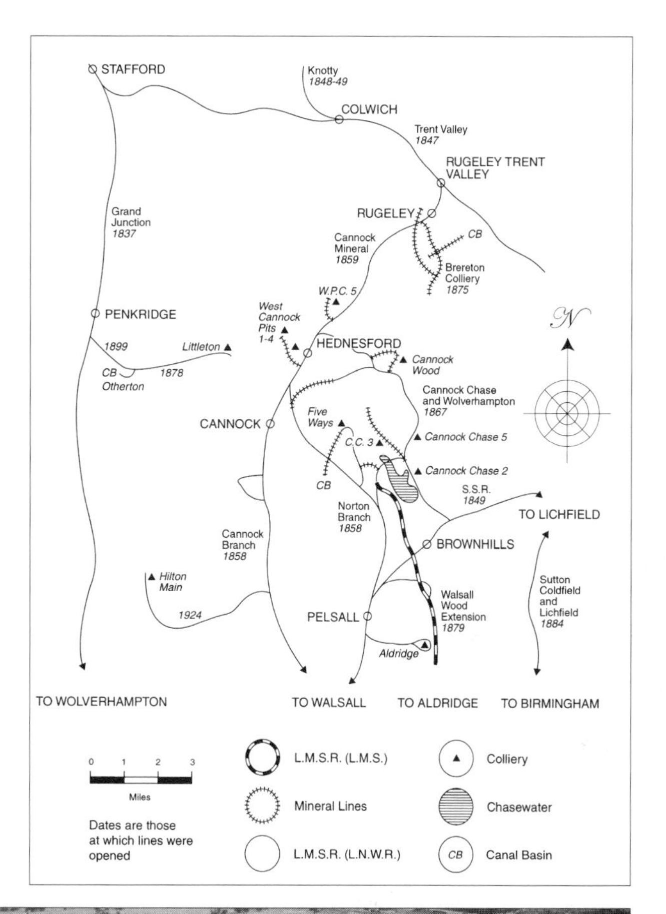

41 The coming of the railways finally ended the isolation of the Chase. Even so, it is unlikely that the line from Cannock to Rugeley would have been built had it not been for the need to transport coal. A complex system of mineral lines also evolved to move coal from individual collieries to collection points such as the East Cannock Canal Basin.

42 Road, Canal and Rail, an aerial view of Bridgtown and beyond. The A5 at Churchbridge junction is in the far distance, as is the line of the Cannock Extension Canal. The Rugeley to Walsall railway line runs behind the new factory buildings around Green Lane. The community of Bridgtown lies just to the right of the A34. The original site of Wootton's timber yard dominates the foreground.

Seven

King Coal

A character in *Brassed Off*, a film about the closure of a northern pit, states 'Coal is history, Miss Mullins.' In other words, the British coal industry, based on deep pits and self-contained mining communities is, for all intents and purposes, finished. On the Chase deep mining ended with the closure of Littleton Colliery, in 1994. Going back only twenty years or so, to say 1975, I doubt whether anyone connected with the area could have imagined such an abrupt end. Nevertheless, in a different sense, coal *is* the history of the Chase. Coal triggered the social and economic development

43 Littleton Colliery in 1994. Littleton Colliery was the last of the deep coal mines on the Chase Coalfield to close. It ceased production after the majority of men voted to accept a pay settlement rather than continue to fight the pit closure. Six hundred employees lost their jobs. What is a more obvious sign of the times than a report in the *Cannock Mercury* that miners would be offered 'counselling' on how to deal with their redundancy?

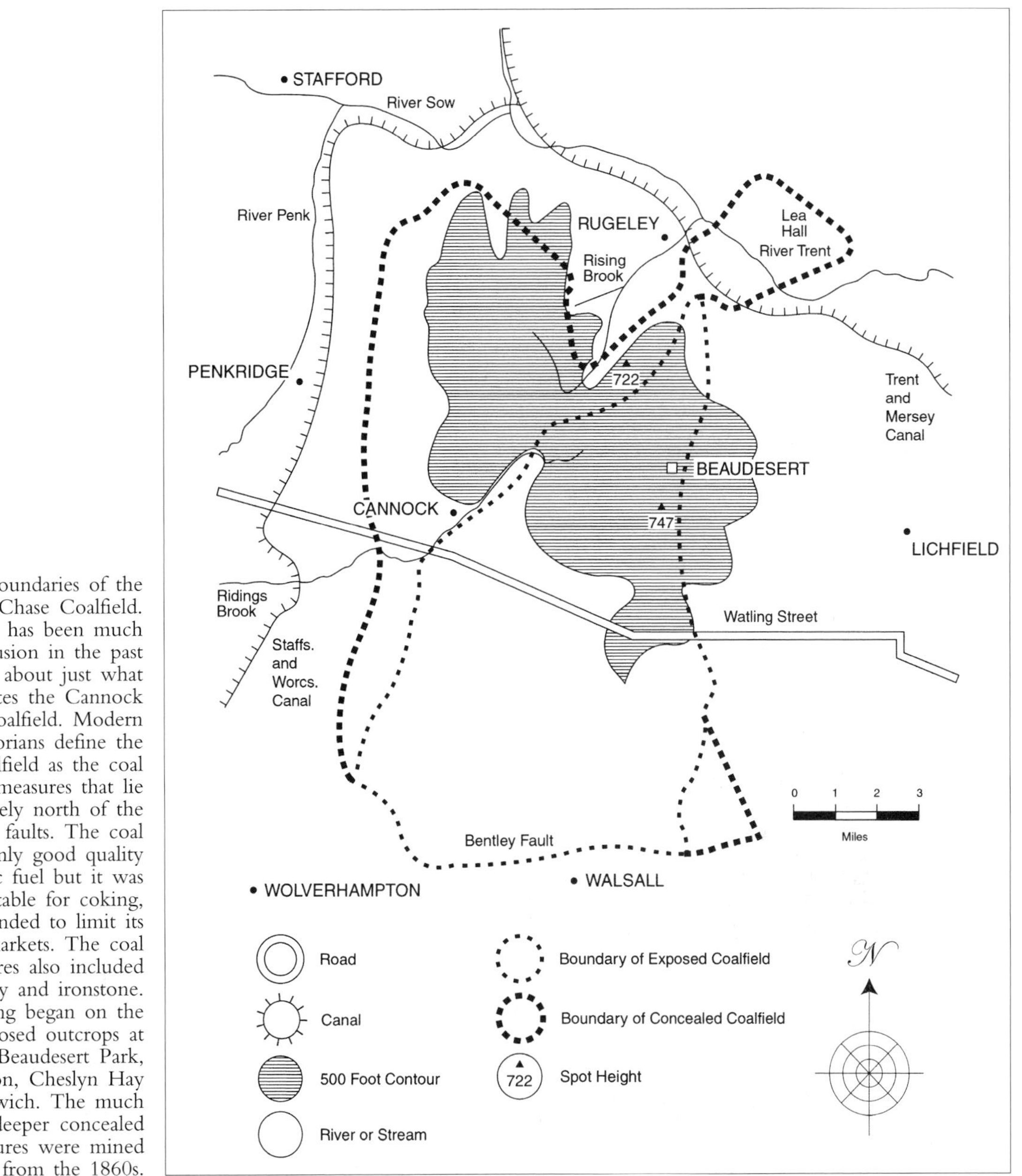

44 The boundaries of the Cannock Chase Coalfield. There has been much confusion in the past about just what constitutes the Cannock Chase Coalfield. Modern historians define the coalfield as the coal measures that lie immediately north of the Bentley faults. The coal was mainly good quality domestic fuel but it was unsuitable for coking, which tended to limit its markets. The coal measures also included clay and ironstone. Mining began on the exposed outcrops at Beaudesert Park, Brereton, Cheslyn Hay and Bloxwich. The much deeper concealed measures were mined from the 1860s.

of the area during the last one hundred and fifty years. Without 'King Coal' the Chase would have a very different story to tell.

The term 'Cannock Chase Coalfield' has changed over time. For much of the 19th century it was considered to be merely an extension of the South Staffordshire Coalfield – which boasted the fabulous 'thirty-foot seam'. By 1880 the Chase had its own Independent Coal Owners Association, and by the 20th century the Cannock Chase Coalfield had become a separate entity, with the Bentley faults marking the boundary between the two fields. In mining terms, Cannock Chase had come of age. The Chase coal measures also include

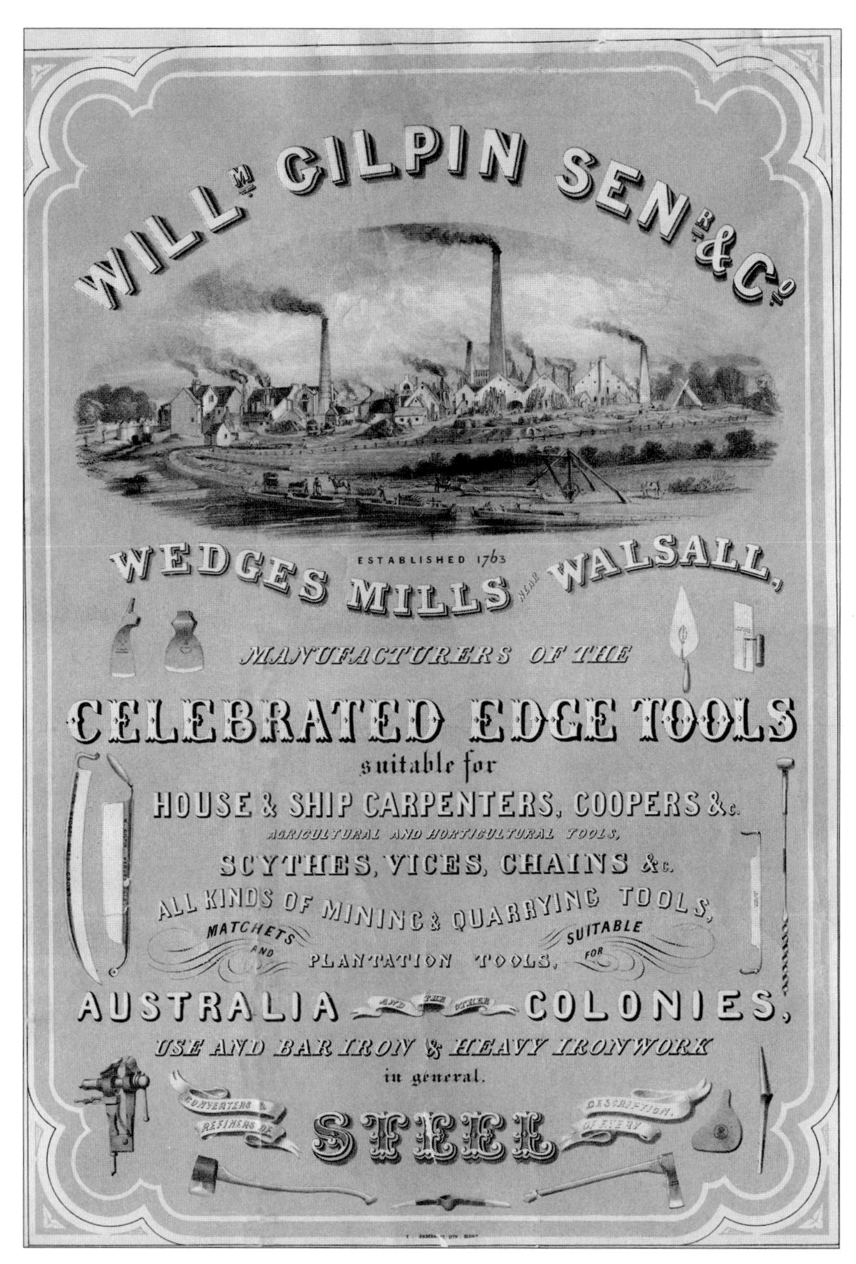

45 Early poster advertising William Gilpin's edge tool company. William Gilpin was apprenticed to Dan Fieldhouse of John's Lane, Wolverhampton in 1770. After serving part of his apprenticeship at the London Docks, Gilpin set up in business in Wolverhampton. He made augers. He married Fanny Bradney and her father gave them the old corn mill known as 'Wedge's Mill' near Cheslyn Hay. He began making blades and augers in 1789. As his business expanded he persuaded skilled workers to move from Gloucestershire and work at his factory. He made his fortune supplying edge tools to the British Empire. He died in 1834.

clay and Gubbins ironstone. The coal is low in sulphur and made excellent domestic fuel. The clay was a valuable commodity because of the high demand for Staffordshire blue bricks – the bane of many a modern DIYer! Locally, these bricks were made at Rumer Hill and Littleworth, and the brickworks were an important part of local industry.

Records indicate that coal outcrops were being mined at Cannock Wood in the 13th century, so why did it take so long to open up the Chase coalfield? There are several reasons. Firstly, the coal was unsuitable for smelting and, secondly, existing methods of transport skirted the Chase rather than crossed it. However, the proximity of the famous 'thirty-foot' coal seam of the Black Country was

46 Gilpin's 'Company Buildings', Wolverhampton Road, Wedges Mills. Situated between the old canal bridge and the brook bridge, they were some of the last 'back to back' housing to be demolished in the district. The houses were pulled down in the 1950s when the road was widened.

the main reason; why attempt to mine an isolated, badly faulted area when so much good quality, cheap coal lay nearby? Nevertheless, coal was mined for local use, and the Pagets did make unsuccessful attempts to reach wider markets. By 1600 bell pits at Beaudesert had been replaced by deeper pits, complete with headings. In 1641 a profit of £472 was made on coal from Beaudesert. Similar returns came in during the 18th century from the Park Colliery at Cannock Wood. The family clearly hoped to exploit these reserves when in 1771 the estate commissioned James Brindley to survey a branch, from the Trent and Mersey Canal to the Park Colliery, but the branch was never built and the Park Colliery closed in 1816.

The first half of the 19th century saw a series of false starts, overly ambitious projects and many disappointments as individuals attempted to sink bigger pits. The risks were often too great. Technology was primitive, flooding was a particular problem and cheap and reliable transport still some way off. Consequently, efforts were limited to the exposed parts of the coalfield at Rugeley and Brereton to the north, and around Great Wyrley and Cheslyn Hay to the south. William Gilpin was one of the pioneers, mining at Colepit Field, Great Wyrley, which he leased from a local farmer, a Mr. Brown. By 1800 he had 36 miners working the pit, which boasted one of the 'new-fangled' Watt steam engines, used to haul the coal up the shaft. Gilpin's coal ensured the viability of his edge tool works, newly opened at Churchbridge. He was one of the most successful of the early independent entrepreneurs of the Chase. Others failed. In 1828

47 William Gilpin's edge tool works at Churchbridge, *c.*1925. Gilpin opened a second factory at Churchbridge in 1806. The new works was powered by steam rather than a water mill. By 1820 Gilpin apparently monopolised the edge tool industry across Britain. Only Sheffield managed to hang on to its cutlery industry. By 1860 the company offered over a thousand different tools for sale.

Joseph Palmer, father of the 'Poisoner', took over one of the Marquis's mines, the Hayes Colliery at Brereton. Estate correspondence indicates that Palmer expected to make a £1,000 profit annually, if he managed to raise 20,000 tons of coal each year. By 1831 it was obvious that the venture was not going to be a success. Palmer died in 1836. His wife then took over the lease but, apparently, the pit was rapidly deteriorating, and much of the coal was wasted. After a long struggle Thomas Landor, Anglesey's Staffordshire agent, eventually forced Palmer's widow to give up the lease in 1847.

A famous legal struggle – the Rumer Hill Case – between the Marquis of Anglesey and Lord Hatherton provides a glimpse of why the aristocratic owners of the mineral rights to the Chase were eventually eclipsed by more astute men. Instead of coming to an amicable agreement over their respective rights to coal at Rumer Hill they wasted a great deal of time and money in the courts, and succeeded in closing the pit as a result. Anglesey gained a technical legal success and Hatherton was able to claim the moral high ground. The miners lost their jobs. Most of the land at Rumer Hill and Leacroft was owned by copyholders. Lord Hatherton had 156 acres of this copyhold land and sank a 220-foot pit on it, around 1835. Hatherton did not ask permission from the lord of the manor, the Marquis of Anglesey, as he thought local custom permitted him to mine freely, as had happened at Great Wyrley.

48 Henry William Paget, Earl of Uxbridge and Beaudesert, had command of the whole of the cavalry and horse artillery in Wellington's army at the Battle of Waterloo. Soon after the battle, in which he had part of his leg blown off, he was created the Marquis of Anglesey. Losing limbs ran in the family. By 1819 his brother, a navy captain, had lost an arm, his son was on crutches having been wounded in the knee and his daughter had lost her left hand during a battle in Spain. He returned to a hero's welcome on the Chase when 10,000 people lined the route from Lichfield to Beaudesert to greet him.

49 Lord Hatherton was born Edward John Walhouse and he adopted the name and arms of Littleton when he inherited his great uncle's estate in 1812. A Tory MP for Staffordshire, he nevertheless voted for the 1832 Reform Bill and was regarded as having betrayed the landed classes by some in his party. His great uncle's main residence was Teddesley Hall. It is said he decided to move to Hatherton and take that title rather than be known as 'Lord Teddy Sly'.

Now although Great Wyrley was only a mile or so away, it was a different manor, and that made all the difference. Establishing the rights to mining copyhold land was anything but clear cut. Copyholders could only mine coal for their own use, but mineral rights owners could not mine the coal unless he or she had the copyholder's consent.

Once Hatherton's mine was up and running Anglesey sought redress. In 1839 he demanded 50 per cent of the royalties. Hatherton's solicitor advised his client to obtain a licence from Anglesey but Hatherton was hell-bent on fighting for local copyholder's rights (or so he said). The ensuing trial was held at Worcester and went in Anglesey's favour. Hatherton was outraged and claimed that Anglesey had 'fixed' the jurors who were, in any case, in awe of the reputation of the great hero of Waterloo and friend of the Duke of Wellington. Hatherton's appeal also failed, and he abandoned the Rumer Hill mine rather than compensate Anglesey. The problem of bloody-minded copyholders continued to plague that part of the coalfield until 1914 when, after a series of false starts, the Mid-Cannock Colliery Company was finally reopened.

50 Sir Thomas Noon Talfourd, judge of the Court of Common Pleas. Talfourd presided over the Rumer Hill case at Worcester between Anglesey and Hatherton. The case was a *cause célèbre* in 1842 – two noblemen disputing feudal rights! Talfourd was regarded as one of the best judges of his day. Curiously, he kept his case notes in rhyming verse! His opening lines recorded, 'The case I'll lay before you will unfold, Some finer points of copyhold, A tenure which in ancient times was base, But now a Peer may own without disgrace.'

The Angleseys have been described as 'essential catalysts of change' in the industrialisation of the Chase. This is because the estate provided much of the initial investment to open up the deep coal measures, lying between 800 and 1,600 feet. The estate promoted transport developments and ensured that several parliamentary enclosures were enacted. These enclosure Acts not only benefited the area but also gave the estate very favourable rights. For a short time the Anglesey estate became one of the most valuable in late 19th-century Britain, and the most valuable one in Staffordshire.

Between 1819 and 1835 the family enjoyed an annual income of around £76,000. However, it had declined to £52,787 by 1854, and the estate was deeply in debt. The knowledge that the Marquis, as lord of the manors of Cannock and Rugeley, held the mineral rights to much of the central part of the Chase coalfield, must have seemed like manna from heaven. For a few decades, exploitation of the estate's coal reserves reversed the decline in the family's fortunes. By 1883 its income had risen to £110,598, of which £32,203 was money from colliery royalties. But even with the extra cash, some members of the family continued to live beyond their means. In April 1882 the *Cannock Advertiser* delighted in reporting that 'The Petities Affiches, a Paris paper, contains a notice from the Marquis of Anglesea (sic) that he will not be responsible for his wife's debts.' The family must have been the despair of their lawyers and agents. By the beginning of the 20th century the Pagets had become yet another aristocratic family trapped in an irreversible decline.

But such a statement would have seemed unbelievable back in 1850. All the evidence suggested that the estate was moving with the times. Indeed, its management was a complex and professional affair by 1849. Lord Anglesey's organisation was headed by two London agents – Beer and Lowe. The next layer of administration employed 11 agents, including Thomas Landor, the Staffordshire manager, and Walter Landor, the Chase area law agent. John Darling was steward of Beaudesert. Thomas Landor and John Darling supervised an accounts assistant, a mineral agent, the Beaudesert bailiff, the domestic establishment at Beaudesert, the mines manager (Francis Figgins), rent collectors and all those who worked at the Hayes or Hammerwich collieries. Meanwhile, the London agents were also responsible for the Marquis's lands in Dorset, Burton-on-Trent, North Wales and Northern Ireland.

The 1840s and 1850s must have been a very frustrating time for the Marquis's agents and managers. The estate was in debt and demanded profits; the agents and managers were under pressure to deliver. Managing the Marquis's mines seems to have been particularly risky. Francis Figgins, the Hammerwich manager, died of typhus which

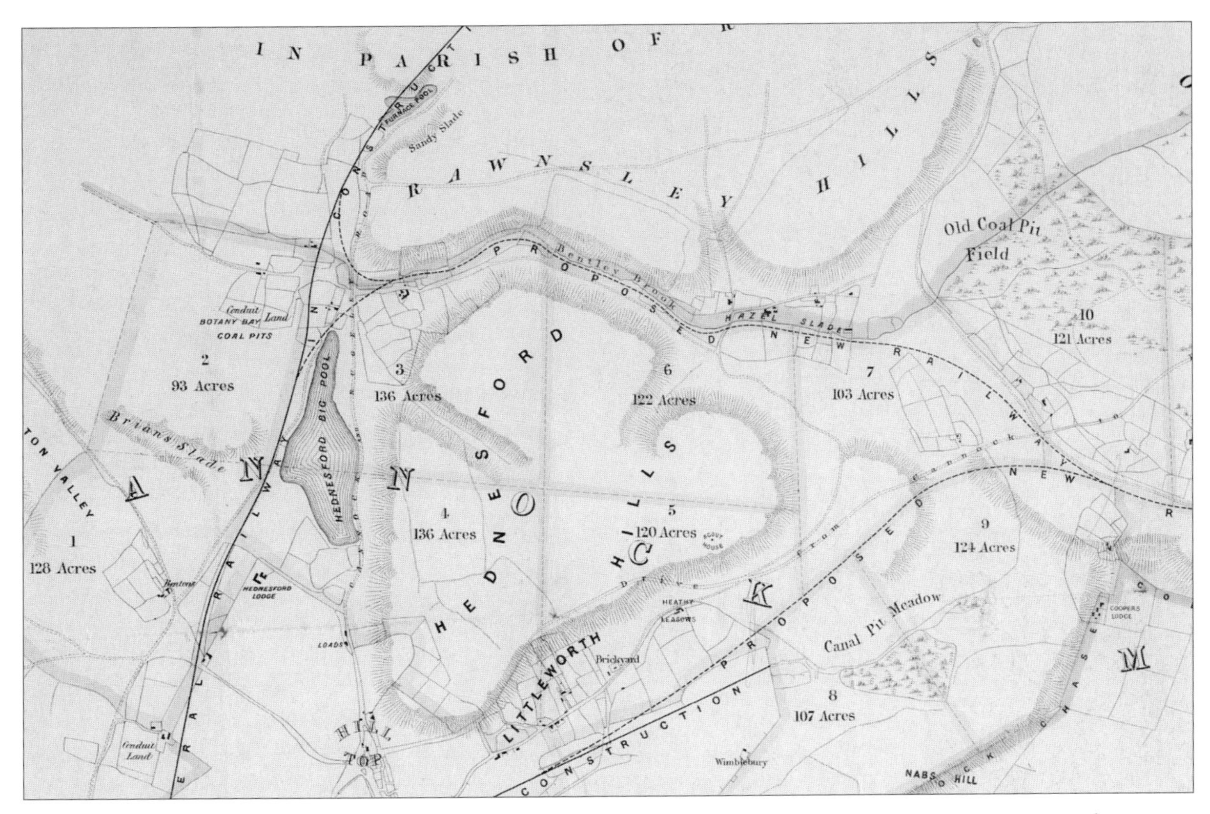

51 During the 1850s the Anglesey estate continued to let further portions of Cannock Chase for mining coal and ironstone. The partnership of Woodhouse and Jeffcock, mining and civil engineers based at Derby, carried out the surveys.

Landor thought had been brought about by 'having too great a weight of business on his hands' – stress is nothing new! Figgins' replacement, Smith, died within four months and so did the underground manager.

For a short time the Hammerwich pit seemed to promise a bright and profitable future for the Anglesey estate. By March 1841 Thomas Landor was planning to end Mrs. Palmer's lease of the Hayes Colliery and thereby free the estate of its guarantee not to open up new pits in competition with the Hayes. Landor employed an experienced and knowledgeable mineral agent from Lancashire named Stott to select a site for a new mine. Stott identified two sites at Hammerwich. Test borings proved the coal to be there but, equally important, the site was also close to the BCN system and, therefore, wider markets. Landor had all sorts of difficulties to overcome before the Hammerwich Colliery was completed and producing coal in August 1851. Unfortunately, this could not have happened at a worse time. The Black Country iron industry was in recession after a run of very good years between 1842 and 1846. The elderly Marquis was in poor health and plagued by his son's extravagance. Cash flow problems were so bad that Francis Figgins was making despairing requests for money to pay the miners' wages shortly before his death.

By March 1852 urgent action was needed. Lord Hatherton advised Anglesey to let his mines so that he could get an immediate income. Hatherton wrote in his journal, ' … a long conversation with Lord Anglesey about his mines, which I hope to induce him to let.' Thomas Landor was suspicious of Hatherton's motives and urged caution before going ahead with the lease. It would appear that Hatherton did not think much of the Landors whom he described as 'deadwood' and 'utterly unfit to do

52 John Robinson McClean was born in Belfast in 1813 and trained as a civil engineer. He lived and worked in London during the late 1830s and 1840s and soon established a reputation as an able engineer and an astute businessman. He was actively involved in tackling London's dreadful sewage and water problems, and he was also the driving force behind the very successful South Staffs Water Company. In later life McClean became President of the Institution of Civil Engineers.

53 Pit mound, East Cannock. Mounds such as this one, near Stafford Lane, Hednesford, once blighted the area – an ugly and ever-present reminder of men having to work in the grimmest of conditions underground. Some, such as West Cannock's 'fiery heap', smouldered continually, making every washday a nightmare for local housewives.

any business'. However, the die was cast. In 1854 J.R. McClean, founder of the Cannock Chase Colliery Company, took on the lease of the Hammerwich and Uxbridge pits. The estate lost an estimated £30,000 on the deal. The sale was a turning point in the history of the estate as it marked the end of the family's direct involvement in mining on the Chase. A new era of mining was about to begin.

The Cannock Chase Coal Company was the first joint stock company to be formed to mine on the central part of the coalfield. It also turned out to be one of the best. It was headed by a man of remarkable energy and vision, John Robinson McClean, a civil engineer, who went into partnership with Richard Croft Chawner, of Wall, near Lichfield. The original partnership became a private limited company by February 1859. It was a well-managed and profitable concern and it had the benefit of attracting some first-class engineers, firstly, McClean and later Arthur Sopwith and his son. It was a fortunate coincidence that McClean managed to persuade Sopwith to join the company – moving from Bohemia, of all places, just a few

54 These houses, in John Street, Wimblebury were built for the Cannock and Wimblebury Colliery Company. They were some of the poorest in the area and were in a dilapidated condition by the 1880s. In 1883 the company owned 28 properties. The first thing the Cannock and Rugeley Colliery Company did on acquiring the houses in 1887 was to invite tenders to repair and decorate them.

months before McClean died, aged 60, in July 1870. Sopwith steered the company through some difficult years in the 1870s. He also ensured that the company were leaders in technological developments. One of their pits, the 'Fly'(No.2), is supposed to be the first in the world to have been lit underground by electricity, in 1882. Many other improvements in safety and efficiency followed. In time, Sopwith's son, Shelford Francis, became general manager until his retirement in 1931.

Other colliery companies followed hard on the heels of the Cannock Chase Company during the late 1860s and early 1870s. Railways, as well as canals, made it possible to transport coal to distant markets. Furthermore, the South Staffordshire field was in decline, ravaged by wasteful, primitive and inefficient methods. Confidence in Chase coal, for a few short years, was high. Silly risks were taken when companies actually sank a shaft before proving the coal was there. This is why Fair Oak Colliery lost £100,000 when its original sinking hit a 'wash out' (a coal bed eroded away and filled with sand). The original East Cannock Colliery Company drew its first coal in 1874 but superficial checks had failed to reveal the disastrous 80-yard fault. This, and poor trade, bankrupted the enterprise in 1880.

The East Cannock directors' minute books paint a vivid picture of an over-stretched venture lurching from crisis to crisis. They sold off valuable housing stock at one point, at a time when homes were desperately needed to

55 Sinking of a Littleton Colliery pit shaft, 1898. The 'cabin boy' on the left was D. Hawkins, the electrician on the right, W. Edge. Tipping the 'bowk' back left, H. Allsopp, back right W. Jaklington (?), front left H. Webb, front right F. Kendrick. The position of the house in the background suggests that the shaft was sunk on the site of what became the pithead baths; in other words on the opposite side of the A34 to where the modern pit stood.

56 Two underground scenes, typical of the conditions in many Chase pits before the advent of mechanisation. The first caption reads 'hand holing' and the second says 'deputy testing for gas'. The working conditions speak for themselves.

accommodate the influx of workers in the 1870s. The directors also refused an application by a local Wesleyan minister, Rev. E. Burton, to make a donation towards the erection of a chapel and schoolroom (in contrast with the Cannock Chase Colliery Company which actively supported such community enterprises). In January 1877 they voted to reduce colliers' wages by 6d. a day (in 1872 it was noted that wage costs were out of hand – rising from 5s. 8d. to 6s. 6d. per shift!). Then on 31 August 1877 came a gas explosion that killed four boys and four horses, and seriously injured another man and boy. The directors sent their sympathies to the bereaved but not much else. They even haggled about the doctor's fee of £20. By September 1880 the original company was finished. The new owner was a Mr. Pochin, a merchant of Bodnant Hall, Conway. Worries about the threat of gas continued and in October 1882 new heads were driven to improve the airway. A small amount of ironstone was raised from time to time – £37 12s. worth in 1881. At the end of 1885 the colliery recorded a modest profit of £3,781 1s. 7d. The company remained near the bottom of the league, in terms of profits and safety, until it closed in 1957.

57 Underground mining conditions, 1955. Very little had changed, except for the electric drill, known as a 'tadger', and the black 'Oldham' type safety helmets, which were being phased out around this time.

Wages had fallen to five shillings a day at the Cannock and Wimblebury Colliery Company in June 1884, and many miners were either out of work or on short time. This was the same all over the coalfield. A less than sympathetic article on the coal trade in the *Cannock Advertiser* described the extravagant waste of miners who were rumoured

to have been seen drinking champagne from pewter pots when they were supposedly earning £1 a day in 1873. The implication seemed to be that miners should be more like the ant and less like the grasshopper, and save for a rainy day.

The great depression in some parts of manufacturing in Britain caused a dramatic drop in the demand for coal. The Cannock and Wimblebury company, mentioned above, was taken over by the Cannock and Rugeley Colliery Company in 1887. Several other colliery companies were either sold at a loss or abandoned during the 1880s. The situation was exacerbated by the London and North Western Railway up to 1882. It had acquired a near monopoly on transport in the area and ignored bitter protests about its high freight charges and

58 Charlie Jones and his sister, Mrs. Cowley, *c*.1900. Mr. Jones's appearance is a reminder of the constant battle respectable wives, mothers, daughters and sisters must have waged against the grime of the pit – dirty clothes, atmospheric pollution and grubby bodies!

59 Harrison's Number 3, Landywood, opened by William Harrison Ltd. in 1896, at a time when business confidence was returning after the prolonged slump, especially in the coal industry, of the 1870s and 1880s.

60 Changing the head gear at the Valley Pit in 1924. The pit first opened in 1873, during the early 'boom years', when demand, already high during the 1850s and 1860s, had been fuelled by the trade boom following the Franco-Prussian War of 1870. The view is unrecognisable at the beginning of the 21st century. Forestry plantations, demolition and new housing have all played their part. Fortunately there is one surviving link with the past. Part of the Valley Pit site is now the Museum of Cannock Chase.

inefficient practices. Once it had acquired the South Staffordshire Junction Railway and the BCN system there was no competition, except from the Staffordshire and Worcestershire Canal. Local colliery companies had even considered establishing their own rail line to link north and south Staffordshire to break the company's hold.

The problem with Chase coal was that much of it was best suited for domestic use. Therefore demand was seasonal and fluctuated with the weather. However, Chase coal was also deemed to be excellent for firing clay; if the companies could win new markets in the Potteries they could ensure a year round demand for their coal. But this was

61 Leacroft Colliery, Cannock. The colliery was managed by Jonathan Hunter for many years. During his lifetime he was known as 'the father of the Cannock Chase Coalfield'. He gained this accolade as much for his interest in miners' welfare as for his abilities as an engineer and a manager.

62 Mid Cannock Colliery wagon. Although the canal system was used to transport Chase coal around the midlands the railways came to dominate long-distance transport by the beginning of the 20th century. However, complaints from colliery owners about the failure of individual rail companies to deliver on time, or even to return their coal wagons, has an all too familiar modern ring!

not a viable option until freight costs came down. The Midland Railway finally broke the London and North Western's monopoly in 1882, and by 1891 Chase coal was going as far afield as London. Confidence began to return and the next phase of the coalfield's development was imminent.

Robert Hanbury started work on the Coppice Colliery at Heath Hayes in 1892. Lord Hatherton reopened the Littleton Colliery, which began operations in 1904. William Harrison Ltd. was another important company; it opened a new pit called Wyrley No.3 in 1896, and it re-opened the Mid-Cannock in 1914. The Cannock and Rugeley Colliery Company and the West Cannock Colliery Company also joined in the race to modernise and increase production. By 1914 the output from the Cannock Chase Coalfield exceeded both the South and North Staffordshire fields.

As yet there is no full-scale book documenting the history of the Chase Coalfield. It is impossible to do more than provide an outline in this chapter, but all sorts of people left their mark on the industry and, for different reasons, deserve to have their story told and recorded. The following stories of Robert Hanbury and Jonathan Hunter must serve as examples. Robert Hanbury MP was born in 1845 at a time when his family's fortunes were improving. Originally from Worcestershire, the family made its first fortune in the wool trade in the 16th and 17th centuries. Francis Hanbury

63 The East Cannock Colliery. The pit was sunk on land which belonged not to the Anglesey estate but to a family of Wednesbury iron founders and bankers named Williams. In 1862 they purchased a 224-acre estate around the original village of Hednesford for £22,000. Evidence suggests that they intended to mine the land themselves but, after several surveys, thought better of it.

acquired Norton Hall, and a two-thirds share of Norton Canes manor, when he married Elizabeth Hussey of Little Wyrley Hall in 1664. The next two generations of the family promptly lost much of their wealth through gambling and were forced to sell the hall and their share in the manor in 1727. The following three generations turned to trade – anything from farming to managing coal mines to running some well-known local inns, such as the *Wolseley Arms* and the *Fleur de Lys* at Norton. It took nearly one hundred years of careful saving and investments to put the family back on the road to social success. One of Robert Hanbury's great uncles had clearly moved up in the world when he became the treasurer of the 'Great Haywood Association for Prosecuting Felons' – such a group would probably have wide appeal today!

It was Robert's uncle who managed to buy back two-thirds of the mineral rights under Norton Canes Common in 1843. However the title was flawed, and complicated family trusts and legal wrangles between the Hanburys and the Husseys were largely responsible for the delays in, and poor development of, Norton's coal reserves. Robert's father died when he was young. Robert also inherited most of his unmarried uncle's valuable estate as well. His uncle ensured that Robert was raised to be a gentlemen. He was educated at Rugby School. He went to Oxford and then toured India and North America. He became an MP for Tamworth in 1872 (gaining many working-class votes by claiming he was a 'collier's son'). He purchased a landed estate at Ilam, in Derbyshire, in 1875. He later became a cabinet minister, the President of the Board of Agriculture, in 1900.

The Coppice Colliery at Five Ways was 'in thorough working order' by 1896 and made a profit of nearly £4,500 that year. The pit was extended when Hanbury leased adjoining mining rights at Newlands and Leacroft, which helped prolong its

64 Littleton Colliery pit mound, *c.*1950. This was the mound on the far side of Cock Sparrow Lane. Waste was transported by means of a gantry from the pit. Two 10 cwt tubs were fixed on either side of the rail. Two men were employed during day shifts to work on the tip to ensure that the operation ran smoothly. Tipping on this mound ceased around 1954. It has since become a landscaped feature of the area.

working life; it finally closed in 1964. Robert Hanbury died in 1903, and on the death of his wife the estate was sold off. However, the Coppice Colliery, at Five Ways, remained a family concern until nationalisation.

Jonathan Hunter had a very different start in life and he certainly had far more right to call himself a 'collier's son' than Robert Hanbury. Jonathan left school, aged nine, in 1867. He spent his early years in a mining community in Durham. By the time he was 11, and working underground, his family lived in North Wales. He earned 1s. 3d. per eleven-hour shift, and worked six days a week. It was at this time that his father stopped the practice of using the 'girdling chain' – worn by youths around their waist in order to pull coal 'boxes' from the coal face to collection points. Jonathan may well have witnessed such barbaric and degrading scenes.

He was 18 when he came to Cannock, as Leacroft Colliery's overman. He had already worked in Warwickshire pits which were prone to 'gob fires' and Lancashire pits prone to flooding. Jonathan had the reputation of being a serious, hard-working and intelligent young man. He combined further study with his pit shifts and rapidly rose through the ranks of management. Firstly, under-manager then manager, and, finally, managing director in 1913. Jonathan Hunter achieved over sixty years of local service so it is no wonder he was referred to as 'the father of the Cannock Chase Coalfield'. He gained this accolade as much for his interest in miners' welfare as for his abilities as an engineer and manager. As with other mining families, his son, T.P. Hunter, became a director and general manager of Leacroft Colliery.

Hanbury and Hunter did very well out of coal. Many thousands of others were not so fortunate. The average miner was extremely lucky if he never had a serious accident during his working life. Even more had their health ruined prematurely – respiratory diseases were killers; rheumatism, nystagmus and deafness, all miserable conditions which marred middle age, were the results of working in water, poor light and alongside loud machinery.

Worst of all were the fatal accidents. The fear and misery associated with such events are, thankfully, beyond the imagination of most people at the start of the 21st century. Let the following list be a reminder of the true cost of coal:

West Cannock No.2 Pit – 1 June 1882, Alex Downes crushed between buffers, only worked two weeks, aged 14.

Cannock Wood Colliery – 14 February 1883, F. Matthias, crushed by fall of rock in stall, aged 67.

East Cannock Colliery – 7 April 1892. Jim Burns and Jim Davies, gassed in gob fire, aged 59 and 21.

65 The Brickworks, Hednesford, now the site of Jewson's and Keys Park. The chimneys once dominated the local landscape. Brick and tile making firms provided one of the few alternatives to mining for working boys and men during the heyday of the Chase Coalfield. It was also part of the site of the original Hednesford Colliery, which was sold to J.R. McClean in 1870. It is sometimes wrongly referred to as the Uxbridge Pit, which was, in fact, situated near Norton Pool, Chase Terrace.

East Cannock Colliery – 3 October 1894, Solomon Woodall, killed in gas explosion caused by a candle, aged 34.

West Cannock No.4 Pit – 3 December 1895, Alf Wilde, fell off railway wagon, caused blood clot, aged 14.

Wimblebury Colliery – 9 October 1902, Jim Morgan caught up in screen machinery, aged 67.

West Cannock No.5 Pit – 1 July 1914, Noah Davies, crushed by coal fall at coal face, aged 41.

Wimblebury Colliery – 14 June 1927, John Wilkes and Bill Harrison, cage crashed to pit bottom, both aged 37.

Cannock Wood – 20 October 1939, George Rowley, fall of rock, aged 57.

Valley Colliery – July 1942, Albert Ryan, hit by runaway tubs in East Deep Hill, aged 48.

West Cannock No.3 Pit – 22 August 1947, George Thacker, killed by fall of rock in roadway, aged 45.

George Thacker died the year the coal industry was nationalised. On Cannock Chase, in 1947, there were 22 working pits, using 33 shafts. There was also one working drift mine. Today the only reminder of coal mining on the Chase is the vast opencast site at Bleak House, between Heath Hayes and Chase Terrace. It may be an eyesore but it is certainly a much more humane way to win coal.

Eight
Matthias Willington Stringer

Matthias Willington Stringer was born in Cannock in 1836. King William IV ruled Britain, the Industrial Revolution was well under way, steam trains were already threatening the canal system; but most local people still lived the unhurried lives of a pre-industrial age. Many of the vast influx of new folk seeking a livelihood from Chase coal had yet to be born, let alone settle in the area. Matthias's family belong to 'Old Cannock'. His mother's maiden name was Benton; her second husband was Edward Willington, whom she married in 1845. All three are local family names whose links with the area have left their mark. Old maps show 'Stringer's meadow' at Rumer Hill, which probably belonged to Thomas Stringer of Leacroft in 1666. 'Benton's Memorial Clock' still stands in Cannock

66 The original Hemlock Farm. The mother of Matthias Willington Stringer lived at Hemlock Farm before her marriage. The farmhouse was demolished in the early 1950s when subsidence made it unsafe. The farmhouse which replaced it is now surrounded by modern housing, built in the 1980s and 1990s.

67 Emma Stringer (née Harvey, of Hednesford), widow of Matthias Willington Stringer. Emma is sitting outside Old Fallow Cottage which was built between 1856-8 by her husband, then a young man in his twenties. Many of the original features of the house can still be seen today. The railings were erected when the area was enclosed in the 1860s.

68 Emma Stringer, photographed some time after her marriage to Matthias. Her clothes are well tailored and smart and the fact that she could afford to have her picture taken indicates that the family were comfortably off thanks to their hard work and thriftiness. Emma was an excellent needlewoman and probably made the clothes herself.

town centre. One of the bells in St Luke's church bore the name Joseph Willington: 1747.

Matthias's father died, aged only 20, when his son was four months old – not the best start in life. Nevertheless, Matthias, a bricklayer by trade, had married and built his own house by the age of 22. It still stands today. Known as Old Fallow Cottage, it is much as it was when it was built in 1858. It is a special building in several respects. It is still owned by Matthias's family, who have the original building accounts. The cottage also has links with the Marquis of Anglesey, just at the time when his family's 'feudal' hold over the area was beginning to decline. It is a quaint and well-preserved link with 'Old Cannock'.

The cottage was built on land purchased from George Poyner, but because the mineral rights belonged to the lord of the manor – the Marquis of Anglesey – the sale took over a year to complete. The Marquis was touring France and Italy, and the legal document followed him half-way across Europe. As a result, Matthias received a hefty bill from his lawyer, which meant that he could not afford to buy the guttering for his home until a good while later! The irony was that the Marquis had left Britain to avoid his many creditors.

Matthias did much of the brickwork himself, as that was his trade. The accounts show that he paid for other labour: fifteen and a half days for a carpenter at 3s. 6d. per day; eighty and three quarter days for a labourer at 2s. 4d. per day, and fifteen days for a lad at 1s. 4d. a day – a total cost of £14 2s. 8d. There was no 'rounding up' – these men were obviously paid for exactly what they did, whether it was a quarter or three quarters of a day, quite literally not a penny more, not a penny less! The other expenses also have the ring of 'the good old days' about them. The front door, complete with fan light, cost £1, and the frame was 10s. 6d. Two stone window sills were another 7s. 6d. The timber, oak and deal cost £26 16s. 6½d. Total cost: £90 0s. 3½d., not bad for a family home still standing over 140 years later!

A few years later Matthias had the opportunity to buy the land – for £12 – in front of his cottage, when Pye Green Road was realigned as part of the enclosure settlement for Cannock. These 'enclosure roads' can still be spotted today – look on a local A-Z map and contrast the old tracks and lanes, which wind and curve their way across the area, with the uncompromisingly straight lines of enclosure roads. Old Fallow Cottage benefited from the change, others were not so lucky.

The extra land helped support a quickly growing family. The couple had 12 children; they reared nine, three died as babies. Twins Matthias and Emma died just a few days after they were born in August 1858, when Emma and Matthias still lodged with

69 William and Hannah Haywood with their grandchildren, *c.*1880. William and Hannah lived in Stafford Road, next door to the old *Wheatsheaf* (now the *Fern and Fallow*). William was a skilled carpenter and he made the gallery for St Luke's Church, Cannock. One of their daughters, Mary Ann, married Matthias's son, William Stringer.

her parents at Hednesford. The twins' coffin cost 7s. 6d.; it was probably made by the carpenter working on the cottage as it was recorded in the building accounts. It could not have been a happy start when the couple moved into their new home a few weeks later, with their eldest son, George. Emma's life must have been typical of many respectable, hard-working women. Not only was she a housewife but she helped look after the family's smallholding; livestock included three cows, sheep and poultry. She also sold eggs, cheese, butter and home-made pork pies at Rugeley market.

Tales are often told of heroic searches for work, long before men could even 'get on their bike'. George Willington Stringer, the eldest son, is one such person. He walked to London in search of work, not once but twice. The first time he was unlucky and returned on foot. Happily, when he

tried again, he found employment as a tile specialist for a firm making hospital and laboratory equipment. His second journey home was by train, a prosperous man.

It is often said today that there is no such thing as a 'job for life' any longer, as though this was always the case in the past. But this assumption hides that fact that many enterprising people, like George, were resourceful and ready to adapt to new opportunities. When he returned home he took up bricklaying again. Then, long winter lay-offs were a virtual certainty (one winter the family

70 Ada Haywood, sister to Mary Ann, *c.*1890. Ada was a very good dressmaker and altogether a rather glamorous lady as her elaborate hairstyle and intricately worked costume suggests. Ada moved away from the area to work as a cook in private service.

71 A building site, probably the *Royal Oak*, at Cannock *c.*1900. The building in the background is almost certainly the old Forum Theatre. Note the scaffolding held together with rope ties. The man in the trilby, standing upper left, is William Stringer, son of the cottage builder.

72 William Stringer at Walhouse Boys' School, New Penkridge Road, Cannock in 1911. William was the grandson of Matthias Willington Stringer. He is pictured kneeling, second from the left. The headmaster was 'Nappy' Napier Walker. His wife, Margaret, was headmistress of the adjacent girls' school.

73 William Stringer in 1920 as an apprentice carpenter at Green and Bird, Stanley Road, West Hill, Hednesford. William is the apprentice (without an apron) on the right, Wilf Oldfield is the apprentice standing to the left. During the 1930s William re-made the door in the Conduit Head, Cannock, when he worked at Linfords.

74 William Tooth aged 58 in 1935. William lived in Victoria Street, Broomhill, Cannock. He worked at East Cannock Colliery Company. His daughter married William Stringer who worked at Green and Bird. The Tooths were another old Cannock family.

were without wages for 13 weeks), so it is small wonder that George also reared sheep on the land around the cottage with his brother William. They continued with this sideline until the First World War when they were instructed to produce hay for army horses instead – failure to comply meant six months' imprisonment. The sheep went!

The mark of a thrifty family is often resourcefulness. And 'getting on with things' did not stop at 'making ends meet'. As young adults two of Emma's children survived smallpox, a killer disease. They were nursed in the sitting room of the cottage – a sheet soaked in carbolic acid hung inside the door and strawberry netting hung with onions covered the other side of the door. Both were simple but effective remedies to contain infection. Intensive care, then, was as good as the best nurse in the family!

Emma and her daughters were all expert needlewomen, one of the indications of a well-educated woman. Only one of her daughters married. Another, Martha, became house keeper to a vicar in Stoke-on-Trent whilst her sister, Amanda, took advantage of the widening job opportunities for women by becoming a receptionist and dispenser for a Shenstone doctor. Their brothers were all bricklayers: one built the wall around the cemetery in Pye Green Road, another worked on the original mining college in Cannock. Occupations such as these must have supported the lives of many similar local families.

It is remarkable that Old Fallow Cottage and its outbuildings have remained substantially untouched and in such good condition. The fact that fascinating archive evidence has also been preserved is even better. If, some time in the future, the cottage faces demolition, perhaps it could be rebuilt in the grounds of the Museum of Cannock Chase? It is certainly too special to lose.

Nine

The Workhouse

Not so long ago the journey from Cannock to Wolverhampton on the number 21 bus took travellers past the Cannock Union Workhouse, on the Wolverhampton Road. Even in the 1950s it looked a grim, forbidding place. Popular literature represented 'the workhouse' as a bitter last resort – a place of misery, shame and despair. And, judging by the evidence, the one at Cannock did nothing to dispel such fears.

Workhouses of one sort or another have a long history. Public workhouses began in the mid-16th century. It is no coincidence that workhouses came into being almost as soon as the dissolution of the monasteries was complete. Some early workhouses – Houses of Correction – were penal; others simply gave relief. However, because of the expense, they were relatively rare until the 18th century. The process became easier by the 1730s when Knatchbull's Act (1723) permitted parishes to band together to build workhouses. There was one built at Snouts Gap, somewhere near what is now Hunter's Road in Cannock, around this time, but virtually nothing is known about it.

The population of Britain started to rise rapidly after 1750, and so did the number of paupers. By 1776 there were some 2,000 workhouses in England and Wales, with a capacity of 90,000 places. But this was not enough and many parishes continued to rely on the provision of outdoor relief, usually a combination of rates and charity. Locally, there were at least twenty charities supplementing parish relief. Typically, such charities were created under the terms of a will. Often, the income came from rented land. Some distributed money to the poorest at special times of the year such as Christmas or Good Friday; others provided for the regular distribution of bread after Sunday service. Henry

CANNOCK UNION.

STATEMENT

OF THE

CLERK TO THE GUARDIANS

SHEWING THE

Names of Paupers Relieved

AND THE

AMOUNT OF MONEY EXPENDED IN RELIEF,

FOR THE

Half-Year Ended Lady-Day, 1900,

TOGETHER WITH THE

RECEIPTS & EXPENDITURE

OF THE UNION AND OF EACH PARISH,

DURING THE SAME PERIOD.

A. W. CARVER, Union Offices, CANNOCK.

Wakefield:

SANDERSON AND CLAYTON, PRINTERS, KIRKGATE.

75 The Poor Law Act of 1834 aimed to reduce the spiralling cost of supporting paupers and discourage all but the most vulnerable from seeking relief. By 1900 each area belonged to a Union of Parishes which provided both in-door and out-door relief. Cannock's Victorian Overseers of the Poor knew all about public accountability and their twice-yearly reports quite literally documented every penny spent.

76 Cannock Union Workhouse, Wolverhampton Road, *c.*1938. The white house in the foreground was, at one time, the home of the master of the workhouse. All the buildings around it formed part of the sprawling site of the workhouse itself. In later years the complex became the Ivy House and then The Chase Hospital. Much of the site has now been redeveloped.

Smythe's charity, established in 1614, was still giving 12 widows two 1d. loaves each week in 1823. Regular attendance at church was often a condition for eligibility: John Troming (probably a descendant of the earlier Trumwyn family) left the income from land in Cannock to the poor 'who attended divine service regularly'. His charity also paid for three new pews in St Luke's that were being occupied by residents of the original workhouse, at Snouts Gap, in 1823.

But the promise of a few shillings a year and the odd loaf of bread was hopelessly inadequate by the end of the 18th century. Agricultural wages were often below subsistence level and industrial workers were at the mercy of trade cycles. St Luke's vestry records suggest that the poor of Cannock were an increasingly difficult burden to bear. A new system of poor relief was needed and many felt that drastic measures were required. The legislation in the Poor Law Amendment Act of 1834 was inevitable – it reflected the mood of the time, or, rather, the thinking of those who governed. It heralded an organised, utilitarian approach to the problem – the Act saved ratepayers several million pounds within the first five years, but many contemporaries bitterly criticised its inhumanity.

The Act of 1834 required groups of parishes, known as 'Unions', to establish a central, shared workhouse. In 1836 most of the Cannock area joined the Penkridge Union, which was approved by the Poor Law Commissioners. It covered an area from Brewood to Brownhills. In March 1877 it was renamed the Cannock Union and encompassed 21 other parishes. The shift from Penkridge to Cannock reflected Cannock's growing industrial importance. This may have rankled at the time, but a comparison of house prices in the two towns today suggests that Penkridge has had the last laugh!

By 1900 the Cannock Union workhouse was an efficient, cost-effective organisation. Records

4

List of Guardians of the Cannock Union.

Chairman—THE RIGHT HON. THE LORD HATHERTON, C.M.G.
Vice-Chairman—MR JOHN THOMAS HATTON.

Elected Guardians.

For the Three Years ending April, 1901.

Acton and Bednall ...	...Rev. Arthur Richard Alsop, Bednall Vicarage, Stafford.
Brewood	...Mr. Joseph Cooper, Coven Lawn
	Rev. H. H. Huffadine, The Manse, Sandy Lane, Brewood
	Mr. G. H. Olarenshaw, Brewood
	Mr. William Pedley, Blackladies' Farm
Bushbury	...Mr. Thomas Jones, Bushbury
	Right Hon. A. S. Hill, Q.C., Oxley Manor
	Mr. Charles Humphreys, Oxley
Cannock (Cannock Ward)	...Mr. Henry Bird, Mill Street, Cannock
	Mr. George Gallatley, Bridgtown
	Bernard Gilpin, Esquire, Longford, Cannock
	Miss Julia Maud Gilpin, Longford, Cannock
,, (Chadsmoor Ward)	...*Mr. Joseph Wilson, Cannock Road, Hednesford
	Mr. Stephen Frederick Dangerfield, Bradbury Lane, Hednesford
	Mrs. Grace Grier, Dulce Domum
	Mr. John Rowley, Five Ways
,, (Hednesford Ward)	...†Mr. David Henshall, Green Heath Road Hednesford
	Mr. Samuel Cotterell, Acorn Inn, Cannock
	Mr. William Henry Gellion, Station Road, Hednesford
	Mr. William Kibble, Reservoir Road, Hednesford
Cheslyn Hay ...	...Mr. Thomas A. Hawkins, Glenthorne, Cheslyn Hay
	Mr. George Evans, Cheslyn Hay
Church Eaton ...	...Mr. William Wyley, High Orm, Stafford
Dunston-with-Coppenhall	.. Rev. Assheton Weekes, Dunston Vicarage.
Essington-with-Hilton	...Mr. John Charles Forrest, Holly Bank House, Essington
	Mr. D. E. Parry, The Croxdene, Bloxwich
	Augustus Leveson Vernon, Esquire, Hilton Hall
Hatherton	...Rev. Oswald Mangin Holden, Gailey Vicarage
Huntington ...	...Mr. Samuel Yates, Huntington
Lapley ...	...Mr. Edward Kendrick, Wheaton Aston, Lapley
Norton Canes ..	...Mr. John Fellows, Norton Canes
	Mr. John Holland, Coppice, Brownhills
	Mr. William Masten, Norton Canes
	Mr. William Neville, Norton Canes
Penkridge and Kinvaston	...Mr. John Robert Briggs, Preston Hill, Penkridge
	Rev. W. T. Corfield, The Vicarage, Penkridge
	The Right Hon. The Lord Hatherton, Teddesley Hall, Penkridge
Saredon	...Mr. John Chamberlain, Great Saredon
Shareshill and Featherstone	...Mr. Charles Price, Featherstone
Stretton	...Mr. Percival H. Brewster, Stretton Mills
Teddesley Hay ...	...Edward A. Foden, Esquire, Teddesley Hay
Great Wyrley, Landywood Ward	...Mr. Edward Smith, Fisher's Farm, Great Wyrley
,, Wyrley Town Ward	...Mr. John Thomas Hatton, Great Wyrley
NOMINATED GUARDIAN	...Rev. E. J. Wrottesley, The Vicarage, Brewood

Meetings on every alternate THURSDAY, at 10.30 o'clock a.m., during the months of April to September; and every alternate FRIDAY during months October to March.

* Vice William Dando deceased. † Vice John Cole resigned.

77 The Guardians of the Cannock Union between 1898-1901. The names reflect the growing importance of the middle classes in public affairs, as well as the traditional role of the landed classes, represented by Lord Hatherton.

40

PARISH OF CANNOCK—Continued.

NAME.	Age.	RESIDENCE.	Cause for requiring Relief.	Relief given to each Pauper during the Half-year.	Relief paid in the Week ending 28th March, 1900.	Sums repaid by Relatives.
				£ s. d.		£ s. d.
Turner Elizabeth ...	64	Wimblebury ...	Age and infirmity	2 10 6	2 0	
Tranter Mary Ann ...	72	Mount street, Hednesford	do ...	3 2 6	2 6	
Tufft Dorothy ...	69	Walsall road, Cannock	do ...	3 2 6	2 6	
Turnock Edward wife & 3 children	32 29	Stafford road, Cannock	Spinal disease ...	8 15 0	7 0	
Taylor Richard ...	80	Cannock road, Chadsmoor	Age and infirmity	2 11 0	Dead	1 0 0
Upton Ellen ...	80	John street, Chadsmoor	do ...	3 2 6	2 6	
Westwood Ann ...	82	Station road, Hednesford	do ...	0 5 8	Dead	
Whitehouse Phœbe ...	78	Hill top ...	do ...	3 2 6	2 6	
Whittaker Sarah ..	76	Wimblebury ...	do ...	3 2 6	2 6	
Ward Maria ...	66	Chadsmoor ...	do ...	3 2 6	2 6	
Ward George ...	69	West Chadsmoor	Blind ...	3 2 6	2 6	
Woodhall Elizabeth ...	37	Chadsmoor ...	Widow & 3 children	5 12 6	4 6	
Wright Ann ..	74	Heath Hayes ...	Age and infirmity	2 10 0	2 0	
Walters Benjamin & wife	70 69	High town ...	do	6 17 6	5 6	
Williams Sarah A. ...	34	Mount street, Hednesford	Widow & 6 children	11 17 6	9 6	
Wright Mary ...	77	Hill top	Age and infirmity	3 1 6	Gone to Workhouse	
Walker Selina ...	69	Church hill ...	do ...	3 6 0	2 6	
Whittall George wife & 3 children	27 26	High town ...	Bronchitis ...	0 6 0	Dead	
Whittall Harriet	26	High town ...	Widow & 3 children	5 8 0	4 6	
Williams William & wife	74 66	Chadsmoor ...	Age and infirmity	6 5 0	5 0	
Wells Henry ...	75	Station road, Hednesford	do ...	3 2 6	2 6	
Yates Joseph & wife ...	86 78	Old Fallow ...	do	3 2 6	2 6	
Morris William & wife ...	71 72	Bridgtown ...	do ...	1 10 0	Dead	1 10 0
Haycock Emily ...	40	Mount street, Hednesford	Own illness ...	0 7 0		
Charmer John ...	65	Littlework ...	Conveyance to Workhouse	0 4 0		
Upton Thomas wife & 5 children	32 34	Chadsmoor	Rheumatism ...	7 10 3	6 0	
Wren Caleb	60	Green Heath ...	Pneumonia	0 1 9	Dead	
Bishop Thomas ...	77	Green Heath	Age and infirmity	0 10 0	Relief transferred	
Whitehouse William & wife	69 50	Bridgtown	Cripple ...	6 0 0	5 0	4 18 6
Vale David wife and child	42 32	Huntington terrace	Asthma	3 15 0	4 0	
Simmonds Ann ...	67	Meghie street, Hednesford	Age and infirmity	2 15 0	2 6	
Cox Mary Ann & 5 children	32	Broomhill ...	Typhoid fever ...	0 14 7½		
Wright Joseph wife & 1 child	68 69	Church hill ...	Child's illness ...	0 5 3		
Newell William Henry wife and 5 children	36 32	Huntington terrace	Funeral expenses ...	1 6 0		
Mattox Harriet ...	65	Bridgetown ..	Age and infirmity	0 19 6	Dead	
Mills Elizabeth ...	75	Church hill ...	do ...	2 10 0	2 6	

78 Just some of the names of paupers officially classed as living in the 'Parish of Cannock' and receiving outdoor relief in 1900. Many of the recipients were elderly people. The introduction of a basic old age pension by the Liberal government in 1909 put an end to many such claims for relief.

indicate that everything was measured and recorded. The list of Guardians in 1900 numbered over forty local worthies, headed by Lord Hatherton. The vice chairman that year was John Thomas Hatton of Great Wyrley. But only two ladies, Mrs. Grace Grier of Chadsmoor and Miss Julia Gilpin of Longford, Cannock, belonged to the Board of Guardians, which met twice a month. The workhouse could accommodate 306 residents, including 40 vagrants, at any one time. The master, A.G. Spire, received an annual salary of £60 (the Clerk to the Guardians received £235). Other employees included a matron, an assistant matron, two nurses, a cook, an industrial trainer, a labour master, a carpenter and a vagrant attendant.

Records indicate that not a scrap of food was wasted. Published dietary tables for the able-bodied, the aged and infirm, and three categories for children of different ages, listed ingredients down to the last ½oz. Each pound of suet pudding consisted of 8oz. of flour and 1½oz. of suet, made up with skim milk when available. It was served with either broth, gravy, treacle or sauce. Each gallon of stew consisted of 24oz. of meat, 80oz. of potatoes and 12oz. of onions. Ten pints of tea were made from 1½oz. of tea leaves. The other recipes were no more appetising and there was very little variety

throughout the week. All in all, there was a pretty good incentive to get out of the workhouse as soon as possible. Every inmate was categorised. Emmanuel Weetman – orphan; Isabella Pockett – destitute; Charles Daw – weak intellect; Amelia Body – imbecile; Betsy Hadlington – deserted; John Lester – blindness; Ellen Dennis – pregnancy. All were from Cannock. In some cases, there are records of relatives being asked to contribute towards an inmate's keep.

Despite the intention of the New Poor Law, outdoor relief survived in many parts of the country – a very primitive form of 'care in the community'. All sorts of people 'benefited' from the system. Harriet Brassington of Heath Hayes had a spinal disease; Minerva Brindley of Mill Green, Cannock

79 Lizzie Walker, née Dutton, a stalwart member of the local Wesleyan Methodist Church in Great Wyrley. Respectable church-going women were the backbone of local charitable organisations, especially during times of crisis such as strikes, when the only alternative would have been the workhouse.

80 Elderly employees of the Cannock Chase Colliery Company. These workers are all aged between 65 and 81. Some of these men had probably worked for around seventy years as miners. In the days before pensions it was either work or the workhouse!

81 Not what it seems! The vicar and the stallman. The vicar of Cannock between 1895 and 1905, the Reverend H.V. Stuart, and an employee of the Coppice Colliery, Heath Hayes. They are pictured standing on Leacroft canal bridge. The vicar had spent a week working underground alongside local miners. Such a thing was virtually unheard of and caused quite a stir at the time.

82 The original *Globe Inn*, near to the East Cannock Colliery. Many of the local public houses provided an opportunity for women to organise their own savings clubs. These were often unregulated Friendly Societies, which were, nevertheless, very successful. At the *Globe Inn* a women's friendly society was formed by the landlady in August 1884. A female burial and benefit club was also run by the landlady, Mrs. Jones, of the nearby *Cross Keys* in the 1880s.

was aged and infirm; Thomas Boddice of Church Hill suffered with a diseased hip; Caleb Wren of Greenheath died of pneumonia despite outdoor relief; the Cox family of Broomhill were granted 14s. 7d. when they contracted typhoid fever. The list, just for the Cannock Parish, contains well over five hundred names, but the cost for the half-year was only £935 18s. 11d., which sounds like value for money for the ratepayers.

The idea of 'looking after your own' was still the norm. Each parish had a responsibility towards all those born within its boundaries. The cost of supporting 'outsiders' living in the parish was £121 10s. 0d. in the first half of 1900 – some 45 people, but only seven of them men. The Cannock Union Guardians would then try to reclaim such expenses from the relevant parish. An even sadder list is that of Lunatics and Idiots confined in Pauper Lunatic Asylums. The standard cost for the care of such people was £12 7s. 0d. per six months. One, George Forrester of Great Wyrley, had been lodged in Stafford Asylum for 27 years, since 1873. Many others were also long-term inmates. The only 'occupational therapy' was sheer hard work. Reading between the lines, it seems the able-bodied paupers either worked with the pigs (26 in 1900 with a value of £57) or in the garden, chopped firewood, sorted rags, picked oakum or broke stone. Given the choice there were probably a lot of keen gardeners!

The original workhouse cost £8,500 to build in 1877. The loan came from the London Assurance

83 The *Hazel Slade Inn*. The United Order of Free Gardeners 'Pride of the Slade Lodge' met regularly at the *Hazel Slade Inn* during the 1880s. The Cannock and Rugeley Colliery Company Sick Club also met at the inn. In 1884 the club had over 1,400 contributing members on its books.

Corporation at an interest rate of 4½ per cent; the company lent another £1,600 the following year, on the same terms. However, Bernard Gilpin, a leading local businessman, extended a further loan of £700 in 1886 at 4 per cent interest, and the Loyal Gilpin Lodge of Oddfellows advanced a further £330 to build a laundry and storeroom in 1888. Here is an example of a rapidly maturing community being able to draw on local capital within the space of a few years.

There were alternatives to the workhouse but most of them, other than private charities, depended on foresight and thriftiness. Easy to say but not so easy to do when many of the workers were miners; especially on the Chase Coalfield, which produced mainly household coal. Older residents will recall the local saying 'a mild winter is a curse and a poor summer is a blessing'; in other words the weather directly affected the demand for domestic coal. The better the weather the higher the chance of lay-offs. The high risk of accident, death or unemployment encouraged a culture of Self-Help. Friendly Societies were at the heart of the movement. These societies were defined, in 1855, as ones whose 'object is to enable the industrious classes, by means of the surplus of their earnings, to provide themselves a maintenance during sickness, infirmity and old age'. The strongest of these societies were the affiliated orders such as the Oddfellows and the Foresters. Both had lodges around the area. The Foresters alone had 221 courts across Staffordshire in 1872.

Many friendly societies were local affairs. The Cannock Friendly Society, formed in 1780, was very important. Early editions of the *Cannock Advertiser* urged 'youths and men' to join it in order to avoid 'the parish'. It was well organised and managed, and provided a range of sickness and death benefits, as well as a very popular annual fête in Cannock. There were many others including ones at Great Wyrley, Norton Canes and Hednesford. Quite a few local public houses ran their own clubs. The original *Globe*

Inn at Hednesford had 120 members in 1876, when 60 turned out for the annual meeting despite bad weather. The *Jolly Collier* at Chadsmoor was the venue for a newly established lodge of the Oddfellows in April 1882. Meanwhile, the Order of Free Gardeners 'Pride of the Slade Lodge' met regularly at the *Hazel Slade* public house, one of the relatively few pubs in the area, in recent times, to have avoided being 'Flagged' or some similar fate!

An interesting feature of local friendly societies is the number of women's clubs; there were at least seventeen. Some were associated with churches, for example the Hednesford Church Schools' United Sisterhood Death Society which first met on 19 August 1879. The title sounds rather bizarre today but the death of the breadwinner then could easily bring destitution to a widow with a young family. Several women ran societies from local pubs, such as Mrs. Robinson's West Cannock Female Birth and Burial Society, which met at the *West Cannock Inn* and had 180 members. The *Star Inn* at Wyrley founded a women's club in 1882 to save for medical attendance and funeral expenses. Many of these local societies were probably unregistered and much must have been taken on trust. Nevertheless, they were successful. There is virtually nothing in the local newspapers of the time to suggest embezzlement or fraud.

Compulsory pit clubs, run by the owners but supported largely by enforced contributions from the miners, were less popular. Often membership was a condition of employment. However, such

84 The *Swan Inn*, Cannock (currently Stones) decorated for George V's Silver Jubilee in 1935. The licensee, Charles Martin, must have been a very interesting character. Born in Gravesend, London, he married, emigrated to Australia and worked as a master baker. However, the family returned to England and settled in Cannock and ran the *Swan Inn* for many years. During the General Strike of 1926 (and the long months afterwards when only the miners stayed out) Mr. Martin paid for a row of shops to be built in Queen's Square, Cannock, in order to provide employment for local men during very difficult times.

85 Mr. Martin's shops, Queen's Square.

FRIENDLY SOCIETIES.

ANCIENT ORDER OF FORESTERS.

District Office, Cromwell House, Cannock. District Secretary, Mr. George Weston.

Court, 4611 "Robin Hood," held at Royal Exchange, Bridgtown. Secretary: A. Holmes, 192 Station Street, Cheslyn Hay, Staffs.

Court 5132, "Hednesford and Rawnsley Rangers," held at 144, Church Hill, Hednesford. Secretary: H. Harvey, 443 Rawnsley, Cannock.

Court 5249, "Pride of Norton," held at Foresters' Hall, Norton Canes. Secretary: C. Watson, 15 School Road, Norton Canes.

Court 6104, "Lord Paget," held at Uxbridge Hotel, Hednesford. Secretary: J. E. C. Johnson, Holliescroft, Station Rd., Hednesford.

Court 6411, "Lord Hatherton," held at Cromwell House, Cannock. Secretary: Joshua Payton, Victoria Street, Hednesford.

Court 6422, "Captain Webb" (Voluntary Section only), held at Crown Hotel, Chadsmoor. Secretary: W. T. Bailey, 13 Price Street, Cannock.

Court 6446, "Little John," held at Red Lion, Cheslyn Hay. Secretary: James Heath, 94 Station Street, Cheslyn Hay, Staffs.

Court 9638, "Lady Anglesey," held at Foresters' Hall, Norton Canes. Secretary: C. Watson, 15 School Road, Norton Canes.

Court 9993, "Pride of Huntington," held at Progressive Club, Huntington. Secretary, Hy. Haywood, 433, Pye Green Rd., Cannock.

CANNOCK PARISH SICK AND BURIAL SOCIETY.

Established in 1878. Held at the Infants' Schools, Cannock. Secretary: Thos. Chackett, 14, Dartmouth Road, Cannock.

INDEPENDENT ORDER OF ODDFELLOWS (Manchester Unity).

"Loyal Gilpin" Lodge, Cannock. Held at the Kingsway Hall, High Green, Cannock. Secretary: F. Chackett, 47 Allport Road, Cannock.

"Good Samaritan" Lodge, held at Four Crosses Inn, Hatherton. Secretary: A. Scott, Four Crosses, Hatherton.

LOYAL ORDER OF ANCIENT SHEPHERDS.

Hednesford Lodge, held at 14 Cannock Rd., Hednesford. Secretary: W. Archer, Belt Road, Hightown.

INDEPENDENT ORDER OF RECHABITIES.

BIRMINGHAM DISTRICT:

Local Secretaries: G. R. Farr, 96, West Hill, Hednesford; H. Cliffe, Tenby Cottages, Burntwood Road, Norton Canes, Cannock; H. W. Baynes, 34 Old Penkridge Road, Cannock; W. Davies, 30, East Street, Bridgtown; T. H. Raybould, 187 Wimblebury Road, Heath Hayes; R. Poole, Rhodo Cottage, Cannock Wood, Gentleshaw; L. Farr, 369, Littleworth, Hednesford.

FRIENDLY SOCIETIES (continued).

NATIONAL UNITED ORDER OF FREE GARDENERS.

Bilston, Walsall and Cannock District.

District Secretary: H. E. Yates, 105, Market Street, Hednesford

LOCAL LODGES—

"Jacob's Shelter," held at Swan Inn, Shareshill. Secretary: H Butler, Church Road, Shareshill.

"Live and Let Live," held at Yew Tree Inn, Norton Canes. Secretary: J. B. Cockayne, Yew Tree Cottage, Norton Canes.

"Star of Hednesford," held at 105, Market Street, Hednesford. Secretary: Samuel Watkiss, 105 Market Street, Hednesford.

"Hand and Heart," held at the Royal Exchange, Bridgtown. Secretary: A. J. Cooke, 68 Watling Street, Bridgtown.

Central Female, held at 105, Market St., Hednesford. Secretary: H. E. Yates.

Brownhills, Hednesford and Cannock Chase District.

District Secretary: Edwin Vaughan, Blackfords, Cannock.

"Pride of the East," No. 1276. Secretary, Edwin Vaughan, Blackfords, Cannock.

"Honeysuckle," No. 1296. Secretary: Robert Tipton, 333, Littleworth, Hednesford.

"Dew Drop," No. 1539. Secretary: L. Wood, 1, Stafford Street, Heath Hayes, Cannock.

SHEFFIELD EQUALISED DISTRICT OF THE ORDER OF DRUIDS FRIENDLY SOCIETY.

Crown Lodge, No. 135. Approved Society for National Health Insurance. Held at Crown Hotel, Chadsmoor. Secretary: James Degg, 104, Cannock Road, Chadsmoor. Treasurer: Wm. Littlehales, 167, Cemetery Road, Broomhill, Cannock.

ROYAL ANTEDELUVIAN ORDER OF BUFFALOES.

LOCAL LODGES.

"Cannock Lodge," held at Royal Oak Hotel, Cannock. Secretary, H. A. Spencer, 12 Gorsey Lane, Cannock.

"Exchange Lodge," held at The Castle, Bridgtown. Secretary. H. Linnell, 58 Watling Street, Bridgtown.

"John Wesley Lodge," held at Anglesey Hotel, Hednesford Secretary, A. Rollins, 14 Abbey Street, Hednesford.

ASSURANCE COMPANIES.

Pearl Assurance Co., Ltd. Offices: Over Waterloo House. District Manager: H. Tatler.

Britannic Assurance Co., Ltd. Offices: Church Street, Cannock. District Manager: H. P. Brown.

Refuge Assurance Co., Ltd. District Office: 156, Wolverhampton Road, Cannock. Superintendent: J. Breeze.

Pioneer Assurance Co., Ltd. Representatives: J. Bull, Dartmouth Road, Cannock; T. Warnsford, West Hill, Hednesford.

Prudential Assurance Co., Ltd. Superintendent: A. E. Dingley, Burns Street, Chadsmoor.

London and Manchester Assurance Co., Ltd. Offices: 112, Mill Street, Cannock. District Manager: W. Barnes.

86 Friendly Societies remained an important part of the communities of Cannock Chase until the advent of the Welfare State. This list, from *The Advertiser Directory* (1938), records some of the official registered societies. There were many more unregulated local clubs that were equally important.

clubs were a major source of relief for victims of non-fatal accidents. These clubs also helped to support ventures such as the miners' Accident Home at Littleworth, opened in 1894. The Cannock Chase Colliery Company, which had a good record of ensuring the welfare of its workers, ran an accident fund that included subscriptions from the miners. It was managed by a committee of 14, most of whom appear to have been workers. In 1872 the fund paid out nearly £400 in accident pay, £141 in sickness pay, the doctor's salary of £308, funeral donations of £68, a £20 bonus for permanent injury, hospital subscriptions of £11, nurses' allowances of £12, and 'stimulants for injured men' of £15. Administrative expenses were less than £30, and over £1,000 remained in balance. Other Chase miners, such as those employed by the East Cannock Colliery Company in its early days, were far less fortunate.

Commercial life assurance companies, trade union schemes and even legal redress were, technically, alternative forms of assistance by the end of the 19th century, but none probably matched the spontaneous help offered by local communities themselves. Autobiographical evidence suggests that pithead collections, street collections, rag rug raffles, gifts of food, rough slack or clothing, and offers of shelter were all local conventions. Such 'community aid' is impossible to quantify, but, nevertheless, it was probably a lifeline to many in times of trouble. It was relatively easy for a group of neighbours to rally round and help a family in difficulties but a miners' strike was another matter. In those days a prolonged strike meant real misery and suffering – hunger, debilitating illness and years of debt. Most people have heard of the 1926 strike – a general strike in support of the miners for ten days, and then a bitter and lonely struggle by the miners, which went on into the winter of 1926-7. This was by far the worst of many disputes between

87 Mrs. Martin, wife of Charles, with her grandson Jimmy Rogers, at the rear of the *Swan Inn*, *c.*1937. Pub landladies did much in the way of unpaid voluntary work to help local charities and needy individuals. Everything from raffles and savings clubs to presentation suppers and annual day trips would be organised by ladies such as Mrs. Martin.

88 A float which appeared in the Hednesford Carnival Parade in 1935. Different organisations put a lot of time and effort into these events. Such carnivals not only provided a day's entertainment but also helped to raise money for the local hospital fund in the days before the National Health Service.

89 Mrs. Sally Dunning with her dog, Gypsy, pulling the cart. Mrs. Dunning was a tireless charity worker whose team of volunteers raised hundreds of pounds for the Hospital Fund at successive Hednesford Carnivals. The Hednesford Hospital Committee was up and running by the 1880s. In 1885 the committee collected £32 12s. 9d. towards the total cost of £55 for treating 18 in-patients and 34 out-patients at the Wolverhampton and Staffordshire General Hospital.

the miners and their employers, both before and after nationalisation. Less well-known, but in some ways – locally, at least – even more menacing, was the unrest of 1912, linked to the introduction of the minimum wage. The poverty, hunger and struggle to keep going during the first half of that year must have tested even the thriftiest working family.

April 1912 will be forever linked with the *Titanic*. The *Cannock Advertiser*'s report of the loss of the ship included a reference to the tragic death of the cellist, whose brother lived in Brownhills. Wesley Woodward transferred to the *Titanic* because his ship, the *Olympic*, had been in a collision with HMS *Hawke* a few weeks before. This cruel twist of fate, and all the other deaths, probably changed the topic of conversation in chapel, club, pub and workplace for a week or so. But the spring of 1912 was pretty desperate for thousands of local people too, judging by events reported in the *Cannock Advertiser*. Yet another miners' strike had begun some weeks before. Never the best paid miners in Britain, workers at Chase pits had seen wages reduced to virtually subsistence level. Trade was bad, argued the coal owners; but it's impossible to exist on your pay, replied the miners. The strike which followed saw violent disorder on a grand scale. Thousands of pounds worth of damage was done to Littleton Colliery when it was attacked by a crowd of '6000 persons' who had 'marched in procession' from Heath Hayes, Cannock, Hednesford and Chadsmoor. Superintendent Spendlove had a difficult time trying to stop the destruction. Facing a barrage of glass bottles and other missiles, the police charged with batons and managed to disperse the crowd. Spendlove ordered that 'strike breakers' working underground be brought to the surface but they had to be accommodated at the colliery, with a guard, that night. Fortunately casualties were light. Only Sergeant Cooper of Cheslyn Hay was injured, along with three miners.

The situation became so tense that 500 officers and men of the 1st West Yorkshire regiment, stationed at Whittington Barracks, were quickly moved by rail to Cannock at a few hours' notice. The following week the local newspaper reported that Cannock was a 'garrison town' with troops billeted in the New Hall and the Public Rooms. Their arrival appeared to have defused the situation and only the regimental band seems to have seen active duty, playing on the bowling green each evening to entertain the locals. Half the young ladies of Cannock appeared to wave them off at the end of the week. But then relatively few miners lived in Cannock itself. Perhaps the soldiers might have had a different reception if they had been billeted in mining communities around the Chase. When officials of the Urban District Council and the Education Committee met to discuss relief measures to help starving children they estimated that over 550 children needed to be fed: 121 in Heath Hayes, 300 in Hednesford, 90 in Chadsmoor, 23 in Wimblebury and 18 in Bridgtown – but only six in Walsall Road, Cannock. Each school day these children were given a current bun and a cup of cocoa, except Wednesdays when they received a beef sandwich instead. More than one elderly resident has gone on record to say that some days that was the only food they had.

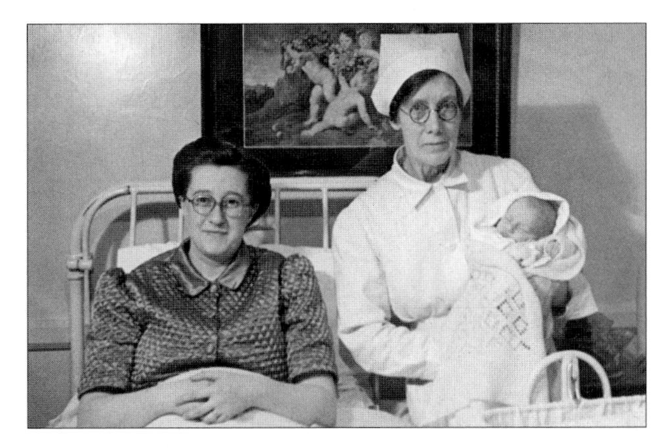

90 Mrs. Spencer and Nurse Phillips. The picture was taken at a private nursing home at Westhill, Hednesford. Such facilities were very limited locally and only available to those who could afford to pay.

Unrest continued into the summer with 120 female workers at Messrs. Moore and Co.'s tailoring establishment, at Hednesford, striking for the right to belong to a trades union and for better working conditions. The girls had a case! They were paid 15s. per one dozen best suits – less deductions for the use of a sewing machine, iron, needles and a stool to sit on! All in all 1912 was a time best forgotten, when the gap between rich and poor had never seemed wider. A whole generation had had the privilege of elementary education but precious little to show for it. That year the spectre of the workhouse hovered over working families like some grim lottery finger. No wonder that there were so many examples of self-help and enterprise to be found. The workhouse is probably the only part of Cannock's past that has disappeared without the slightest regret.

Ten

The Communities of Cannock Chase

The Hearth Tax returns of 1666 for the East Cuttlestone Hundred paint a vivid picture of the communities of Cannock Chase shortly after the restoration of King Charles II. The tax, also called 'chimney money', was introduced in 1662 at a standard rate of two shillings per hearth, which was paid twice yearly, except by those exempted on grounds of poverty. The tax was so unpopular that it was abolished following the 'Glorious Revolution' of 1688-9. It was hated because it was seen as a tax on the poor and an infringement of an Englishman's liberty since it gave officials the right to search a taxpayer's home. From a historian's point of view, the records are invaluable as they can give many clues about social structure and household size.

In Huntington 40 householders were chargeable but, except for George Stubbs who had four 'chargeable hearths', and another six people who had two or three hearths, some thirty must have lived in small (or very cold!) cottages with only a single hearth. Six were listed as exempt from the tax. This pattern is repeated across the other communities of that time. Great Wyrley had 50 chargeable households; Mr. John Allport and John Wilson each had five hearths but most of the others only had one. And quite a few people lived in poverty in Great Wyrley where 25 people were 'certified for not to be chargeable'. At 'Cheslaine Hey' 10 householders are listed, including Symon Brevett who lived in the only house that had two chargeable hearths; all the rest had one.

Cheslyn Hay was a curious place at this time. It was a sort of 'no man's land', being outside the jurisdiction of either a lord of the manor or the Church. It was one of several 'extra parochial' areas in Staffordshire, which had not been incorporated within a parish. This strange position was compounded by the fact that it was classed as a 'hamlett' of Sheriffhales, in Shropshire, for administrative

Leacroft.

	[Hearthes Chargeable.]
Edward Byrche, Esquire	Fifteen
Thomas Stringer	Five
William Fletcher	One
Edward Fletcher	One
Walter Byrche	Two
William Salt	One
John Lard	Three
Robert Reynoldes	One
Richard Hart	One
William Worthington	Five
Edward Perkins	Two
Thomas Dorrington	One
Edward Hart	Two
John Deakin	Three
Edward Rowley	Two

91 Transcription of the Hearth Tax returns for Leacroft.

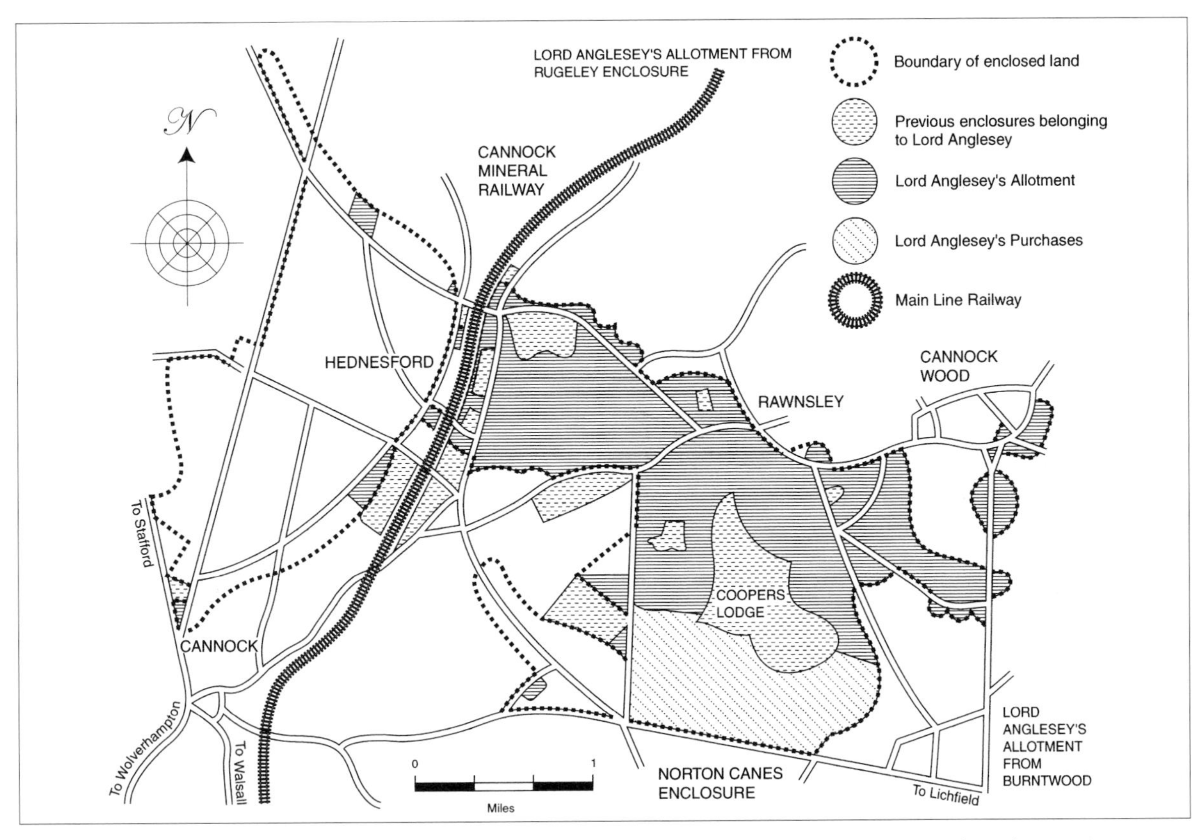

92 The Cannock Enclosure Award. The award protected the mineral rights of the Marquis of Anglesey and it ensured that a network of new roads opened up the area to entrepreneurs ready to exploit the new coalfield.

purposes. The common links seem to be the Leveson family, who owned parts of Cheslyn Hay and Sherriffhales, and the fact that Sherriffhales was part of the Cuttlestone Hundred. It probably all seemed perfectly logical at the time.

In nearby Hatherton John Walhouse had five hearths and was listed as a 'gentleman'. Generally, Hatherton appears to be a more prosperous township as far fewer of the 28 taxable homes had only one hearth, and just nine were listed as too poor to pay. The record of 'Cannock Constablewick with its hamletts' indicates a high level of poverty, however. Cannock itself had 44 chargeable homes. One, belonging to Mr. John Byrche, had 'eleaven' hearths, and other homes listed as having anything between eight to one hearth suggest a small town supporting a range of occupations, rather than a village sustained only by agriculture. However, there were also 42 households living in poverty.

The 'hamletts' of Cannock comprised Leacroft, 'Hedgford' and 'Cannockwood'. Leacroft Hall boasted 15 hearths and was owned by Edward Byrche, Esquire. Leacroft had 15 householders paying the tax and a further nine who did not. At 'Hedgford', 38 homes were chargeable, the largest, belonging to Mr. Charles Colman, had 'nyne' hearths but the house was listed as 'demolished and sould'. He and his family were devout Catholics who had paid heavily for their faith; several records survive which describe the family as recusants, often fined for their religuos beliefs between 1607 and 1641. Charles Colman was convicted again in 1667, some of the proceeds of the land sale possibly helping to pay the fine. Another 15 living in 'Hedgford' did not have to pay, including the quaintly named 'Widdow Tingle'. At 'Cannockwood' 18 were exempted from paying the tax. The two local constables for Cannock who carried out this

93 Littleworth Road, Rawnsley, some of the earliest colliery houses built in the area. Erected in the 1870s on leasehold land which belonged to the Marquis of Anglesey, they were valued at £91 each in 1947.

94 Simcox Street, Hednesford, probably named after the much-maligned builder, Robert Simcox. These houses stood at the top of Church Hill. The complete row was sold in March 1946 for £445. The first vicar of Hednesford stated that houses such as these, which overlooked St Peter's church, were a 'great affliction' to him.

unpopular survey were Henry Tymminges (perhaps a descendant of the medieval Trumwynes?) and Thomas Willington, an ancestor of Matthias Willington Stringer whose story is told elsewhere in this book.

Norton Canes and Little Wyrley were part of the Offlow Hundred and so their records were kept separately. Three years later, in 1669, these two communities had 23 households classed as chargeable; only Ferrars Fowke had six hearths and John Moss had three, all the rest were cottages with one or two hearths. No doubt others were exempted from paying.

These, then, were the ancient communities of the central and southern parts of the Chase. And as long as the population remained relatively stable there was little need to expand. However, from time to time there were 'great leaps forward' which saw changes in settlement patterns. These were marked by enclosures of one sort or another. Early land enclosures were often done to convert open arable fields to sheep runs, and were carried out by the local lord without any consultation. By the 17th century enclosures were more likely to be carried out by agreement between the lord of the manor and copyholders. In 1668 Robert Leveson, lord of the manor of Great Wyrley, enclosed 600 acres of common land for cultivation in this way. The third type of enclosure was that implemented by an Act of Parliament. Such Acts were at their height between 1755 and 1815 and the motives behind them were many and complex. They enabled the main landowners to obtain the enclosure of a given area whether or not all the lesser owners agreed. Without these acts, in the Midlands in particular, it would not have been possible to create all the new communities needed to accommodate the rapidly growing population from the 1750s onwards. Parliamentary enclosures were an expensive business and the timing of them usually coincided with favourable economic conditions, which would mean that related costs could be recouped.

Parliamentary enclosures came late to the Chase. Cheslyn Hay saw the earliest, in 1797. One of the main motives for enclosing land here was tackling the high level of pauperism, which was aggravated by the rapidly rising population and by squatters encroaching on waste land. But the enclosures that followed were based on the intention to protect mineral rights and open up access to the coalfield. Hammerwich was enclosed in 1856, Hatherton in 1859, Burntwood and Longdon in 1861, Cannock and Norton Canes in 1868 and, finally, Rugeley in 1885. Much has been written about the reasons behind enclosure and its subsequent effects. Motives were complex and modern research indicates that the results often created more winners than losers. This was certainly the case when parts of Cannock were enclosed. The Anglesey estate did very well, but so did many other smaller landowners. A sound infrastructure was established and land became available for housing. Enclosure ensured that the area was ripe for development. By 1863, 60 miles of road had been built at a cost of £24,000. Other roads followed, all paid for by the sales of enclosure allotments. Cheslyn Hay was unique locally, as it had no lord of the manor. Therefore the mineral rights went to the new surface owners, but in almost all other cases the lord of the manor benefited: either the Angleseys, the Hanburys or the Husseys. The Marquis conceded his mineral rights at Hammerwich but at Cannock, Burntwood and Rugeley, he kept the rights to all minerals, except brickclay and sand. For the Marquis it was a classic example of a landowner using his political power to gain economic advantage.

The enclosures also meant that new homes could be built. Without accommodation for the miners and their families the proposed collieries were unworkable. In Hednesford, for example, there were 45 houses in 1851. By 1891 some 1,042 new houses had been erected. How did it happen? Building land was plentiful and relatively cheap. The Marquis sold his land leasehold; others sold theirs freehold. There were plenty of investors ready to take advantage of the situation. Building materials, except for lime from Walsall, were available locally and Black Country labour and expertise was only a train ride away. Local 'nimbys' at the time must have been horrified as the mines expanded and the new communities mushroomed – the new towns or villages of Hednesford, Rawnsley, Wimblebury, Heath Hayes, Chasetown, Chase Terrace, Chadsmoor and Bridgtown all came into existence during the last forty years of the 19th century.

95 Bank Street, Heath Hayes. Such houses represented the spirit of enterprise in Heath Hayes. Many local miners built their own semi-detached homes. They lived in one and rented the other. The second house either paid the mortgage or acted as insurance in hard times.

Although these new communities were for mining families they were not just 'pit villages', owned lock, stock and barrel by the colliery companies, as in some other parts of England. Sinking a deep pit on the Chase was a very expensive business and some companies decided to leave the challenge to the private sector (another fashionable 'modern' concept that has deep roots).

The Anglesey estate was the first to face the problem of homes for miners. In 1852 one of Anglesey's agents expressed surprise that the estate had 'done so long and so well without them'. Fortunately for Chasetown, the estate rejected the idea of building 'barrack' accommodation for the two hundred miners which the Hammerwich and Uxbridge pits needed, and opted instead for 'model colliers' cottages'. Although the first cottages were deemed 'solid and first-rate', however, only three pairs in Church Road were built – at £60 per cottage they were simply too expensive!

Most local companies developed a policy of providing homes for key workers, such as the manager and engineers in the case of the Cannock Chase Colliery Company. But only two companies built homes for ordinary workers. The West Cannock Company owned 52 houses by 1883. The Cannock and Rugeley Company owned nearly one hundred houses by 1890, and continued to add to its stock until 1926, when it built Prospect Village.

The majority of miners relied on privately rented accommodation. Small-scale investor-landlords dominated the local market, owning 76 per cent of houses in 1890. Records show that many of these lived in the Black Country, which enjoyed a sophisticated, mature economy generating capital for investment elsewhere. A snapshot view in 1883

96 Cannock Road, Heath Hayes, looking towards the 'Fair Lady' corner, Five Ways. The old mission church is in the foreground.

97 Church Street, Cannock. The centre of Cannock remained unaffected by the rapid growth of the coalfield and it managed to retain the appearance of a pleasant country town until the ravages of 'enlightened' civic redevelopment over the last thirty years.

98 Hednesford from the hills. Hednesford Hills was given to the people of the district by the Marquis of Anglesey, including land for the future needs of the cemetery attached to St Peter's church, Hednesford, in 1933.

99 Our Lady of Lourdes, Hednesford. This imposing Roman Catholic church was built at Hednesford and opened and dedicated in 1934.

shows some 163 landlords with between three to five properties to rent; only two owned 21 or more. There were a few enterprising local builders who also became landlords: Hednesford builder David Williamson owned 13 houses in 1883, Robert Barton, builder and builder's merchant of Littleworth, owned 28, and William Simcox, builder, member of the Board of Health and a founder member of the planning committee, owned three.

The first vicar of Hednesford, the Reverend Bullivant, had a pretty low opinion of Simcox. In a letter to Anglesey's agent in 1875, Bullivant accused Simcox of having the effrontery to build 'common colliers' cottages' opposite St Peter's church. Judging

100 Hednesford Road, Heath Hayes, looking towards Hednesford, *c.*1920s. The *Talbot* still exists today, as does the Methodist church. Heath Hayes always enjoyed the reputation of being one of the more prosperous and respectable local communities and there is little in this photograph to suggest otherwise.

101 The premises of George Tranter's, Market Street, Hednesford. He began trading in 1905. Several generations of Hednesford folk have enjoyed the Tranter family's excellent products. And it will be a long time before Paul Tranter's cheerful insults are forgotten. The business closed on 28 October 2000 – the end of an era!

by his second, very conciliatory, letter, Bullivant was clearly told to mind his own business. The irony is that some of the original terraced housing remains around the church whilst the church itself has been rebuilt. And to be fair to Simcox, the *Walsall Observer* reported in December 1873 that 'The building of the new Congregational Church at Hednesford is credit to the builder Simcox.' Nevertheless, Bullivant had a point. Much of the housing was shoddy, especially homes built before 1875, the year of the Artisans' Dwelling Act, which attempted to set down

102 Market Street, Hednesford in the 1950s. The new town of Hednesford developed nearly a mile away from the old village of Hednesford, based around the *Cross Keys*. It was the Anglesey estate which promoted the growth of the new town, and the estate retained the leasehold on many properties in the area well into the 1960s.

basic standards for new buildings. Buxton's Buildings, erected in 1875, in Uxbridge Street, Hednesford and still standing today, are a good example of the early impact of this legislation. Private landlords have all too often been regarded as villains – ruthless in their pursuit of rent, but deaf to pleas for the maintenance of their houses. However, the prolonged slump between 1873 and the late 1880s saw unemployment, nationally, rise from a mere one to 10 per cent, and the result was that many landlords were left with empty houses that were soon vandalised, and their single row of homes often represented a large part of their income. This period was a miserable time for many on the Chase and it is little wonder that so many properties became dilapidated.

There was also a significant number of enterprising folk in the area who made the best of whatever opportunities came their way. The community of Five Ways, which became Heath Hayes, is a case in point. By 1890 there were 51 owner-occupiers in the village; many were miners and some even built their own homes. The story of one resident – Albert Foster – typifies the cherished belief in 'self-help', popularised by Samuel Smiles. Foster's whole life is a story of hard work and dogged determination. He began work at one of the Cannock Chase Colliery Company pits in 1879. In 1883 his father died, leaving Albert to support his mother and younger brother. Even so, Albert Foster managed to borrow £150 to build his own house before he was 28, and married. After twenty years as a miner he opened a baker's shop in Heath Hayes, and after another twenty years he brought a farm at Chorley that he worked for twenty years more. He and his wife finally

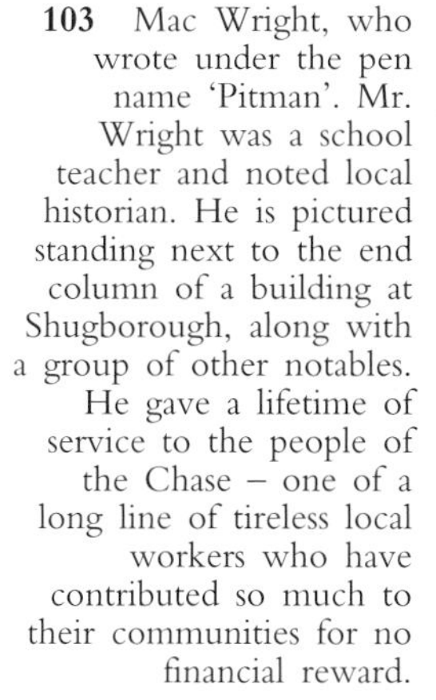

103 Mac Wright, who wrote under the pen name 'Pitman'. Mr. Wright was a school teacher and noted local historian. He is pictured standing next to the end column of a building at Shugborough, along with a group of other notables. He gave a lifetime of service to the people of the Chase – one of a long line of tireless local workers who have contributed so much to their communities for no financial reward.

retired to Bridge Cross, Chase Terrace in the 1940s. Mr. Foster's story is unique in that it was recorded, but there must have been many other 'Fosters' who battled against daunting odds in order to own their own home and improve their lot.

As the number of houses increased so did the facilities. Shops were the first to appear. James Smith of Hednesford, Family Grocer and Tea Dealer, took advantage of the railway network and was selling a sophisticated range of provisions, including Wiltshire hams and American cheese in 1878. Chemists, milliners, dressmakers, cobblers, banks, greengrocers, butchers and bakers, to name a few, were all up and running almost as soon as the first houses were built. Music teachers, undertakers, schools, elocution specialists and barbers placed discreet advertisements in the local newspapers - always offering best value and moderate terms.

There were many problems connected with managing these new towns and villages, not least the provision of services which were essential in an industrial society. The Boards of Health struggled to meet the problems posed by rapid growth, and it was not until the new Urban District and Rural District Councils and County Councils came into being, in 1894, that truly effective management and planning began. The Urban District of Cannock took in the communities of Hednesford, Heath Hayes, Rawnsley and Littleworth. Norton Canes became part of Brownhills, and Great Wyrley and Cheslyn Hay part of the rural district of Cannock. A century ago these new local authorities rapidly acquired a wide range of responsibilities from sanitation to elementary education, health measures to highways and housing. Other public services also came to be a valued part of the community. The 1920s saw the beginnings of free public libraries, an ambulance and a fire service, and a local authority electricity supply from 1922.

Together the councillors and the employees of the local councils, urban and rural, work tremendously hard to transform and improve the communities of the area. These were local people, accountable to local people, who gave a lifetime of service for little or no financial reward. It is very unlikely that local authorities will ever have so many powers, or responsibilities, again. Some would say more is the pity.

Eleven

Leisure, Recreation and Sport

There is a handwritten note in the margin of a *White's Directory* (1851) in Cannock Library which states that John Corns, a local butcher, used to purchase the 'damaged' bulls, maimed by dogs at the annual Cannock Wakes. This is virtually the only evidence that local people enjoyed such blood sports well into the 19th century. The same anonymous hand commented that Thomas Gripton, miller and publican of the *Vine Inn*, Walkmill Lane, was a 'cockfighter all in'. He also, apparently, 'kept a very clean public'.

Cock-fighting was endemic on the Chase. The *Cross Keys Inn* at Old Hednesford hosted many a fight in the 'big room', which apparently had a purpose built cock pit set in the floor. These events attracted large crowds and extravagant betting.

104 Hunting, another ancient blood sport, continued on the Chase. Unlike many other blood sports, it was confined to the ranks of gentlemen and above. Hunting stags was strictly limited to those, such as the Marquis of Anglesey, who still held feudal rights.

105 The *Central Hotel*, Blackfords in the early 20th century. 'The Central' was one of the first purpose-built public houses which had function rooms as well as several bars for its clientele. It was designed to maximise its trade by offering separate rooms for anything from club meetings to wedding receptions.

More often cock fights were staged outdoors. A dip in Hednesford Hills has long been known as 'Cockpit Hill'. Although it was banned in 1835 the 'sport' continued in open defiance of the law. William Sharman, who grew up in Bradbury Lane in the first years of the century, vividly described the fights he witnessed. William was paid a penny to look out for 'the law' and warn the men, by then mostly miners, of police activity. Prize fighting was also common. Bare-fisted fighters would often fight till they dropped. Usually the fights took place outside a public house. There was a fighting ground in the 1850s near to Wharwell Farm, Great Wyrley, which at one time doubled as a beerhouse called 'The Old Engine'. Again, the *Cross Keys* was another popular venue for 'big name' fights.

The Cannock Wakes were the high spot of the year. Described as 'ancient and annual' in 1851, they ran for four days during October. They were riotous affairs, allowing a break from everyday routines before the winter months. All manner of 'sports', games and competitions took place. The Wakes offered a chance to gamble, gossip and relax; the event was part of the old and traditional way of local life.

The South Staffordshire Association for the Abolition of Bull Baiting was formed in 1824. It was an early example of popular pressure successfully persuading Parliament to pass legislation which

106 Hatherton Hall, home of Lord Hatherton who opened his grounds for local Roman Catholics to celebrate an annual fête. Newspaper reports of the time suggest that the fêtes were very lively affairs which attracted hundreds of people.

reflected changing attitudes. Within ten years bull baiting was outlawed. In many ways the 1830s became a watershed between the past and the present. It was a decade of reform – led by the middle classes who were, increasingly, becoming a dominant political and social force. By the end of the century leisure, recreation and sport had changed beyond recognition.

'Drink' was one of the main issues of the century. Methodism and the wider temperance movement persuaded several million to become tee-total. At the same time many public houses were becoming more comfortable and inviting places. What a dilemma! The respectable side of alcohol is reflected in advertisements such as those placed by the Cannock Brewery Company, which offered an early 'beer at home' delivery service to families in 1879. There is also a lot of evidence to show that the police and magistrates did their best to enforce licensing laws. However, one case, against J. Simmons, beer keeper at Wimblebury, was dismissed because of the way the evidence had been gathered when it was found that he served beer out of hours to two 'disguised policemen' in 1878.

Public order was just as much a problem in the 19th century as it is today. There are many complaints from 'ratepayers' to be found in the pages of the *Cannock Advertiser.* Large gangs of 'men and youths' would regularly congregate on the footpath between the *Five Ways Inn* and the *Talbot* in what was to become Heath Hayes, in the 1880s. Their 'loud and threatening' behaviour terrorised other local people. It was no better in Market Place, Hednesford. Local residents often complained about 'drunken singing' and the fact that drunks 'are removing all manner of things and hiding them'.

But for every drunk there was an upright teetotaller. Those who had signed the pledge had a wide range of social activities on offer. The 'Pleasant Sunday Afternoon Club' met at Hightown Methodist Church at the turn of the century and had over 200 members. The Cannock branch of the Church of England Temperance Society went to Llandudno in 1878 – around 500 joined the excursion. The *Cannock Advertiser* reported that

107 A Sunday School Anniversary Parade, marching from Hightown to the Methodist church at Chadsmoor. Some of these occasions would attract literally thousands of people, all dressed in their 'Sunday best'.

several were left behind in Llandudno and Rhyl. Unfortunately the report doesn't say why! The Hednesford Coffee House, situated in Market Street, was offering an alternative to the *Anglesey* and the *Uxbridge* public houses by 1882. Members of the Hednesford and District Total Abstinence and Band of Hope Union regularly had attendances of over sixty at their meetings. Meanwhile the Wesleyan annual tea meetings at Calf Heath often attracted over 250 folk.

Church and Chapel provided many opportunities for 'respectable' leisure activities. And for women they were virtually the only such outlets. The Primitive Methodist Chapel at Littleworth had a thriving choir that put on public performances of sacred music which were well attended. Local Roman Catholics seem to have had a jollier time at their annual fête, held in the grounds of the home of Sir Charles Clifford, at Hatherton. The 500 visitors enjoyed refreshments, football, racing, swinging, coconut bowling, rowing and 'damaging Aunt Sally's pipes'! St Mary's, Cannock, also ran a regular lottery during the 1880s – probably one of the few opportunities to gamble within the law at that time. Again, there are many examples of those involved in illegal gambling being reported, or brought to book. One irate ratepayer from Great Wyrley wrote about the problem in a letter to the *Cannock Advertiser* in 1890. Apparently, Great Wyrley was notorious for such 'goings on'.

Sunday school anniversaries still exist today, although in terms of size and scale they are nothing like those of the past. There are photographs of literally thousands of people packed together in the

108 Methodism played a vital part in the lives of many miners and their families. Almost every community had at least one Methodist chapel. This is Bourne Methodist church, Heath Hayes. Such institutions provided a range of respectable leisure activities, far removed from the temptation of the 'demon drink'.

main street of Hednesford to celebrate the annual Sunday School Demonstration around the turn of the century. Beautiful and intricately made banners identified each group – the occasion called for 'Sunday Best' in every sense of the word.

Mutual Improvement societies also thrived. One was based at the Great Wyrley Institute, another at Hednesford. They offered everything from summer picnics at Shoal Hill to regular lectures. The elocution lessons at Hednesford were particularly popular with 'the ladies'. Lectures covered topics as diverse as *Hamlet*, 'The Lighting of Fiery Mines' and 'Vegetarianism'. However, one Wesleyan Chapel lecture in the 1880s on 'Eminent Miners' drew an 'uncharacteristic' moderate attendance – the report does not say whether it was poor weather or the topic that was the cause!

The Hazelslade and Rawnsley Horticultural and Floral Society was well established by 1890, along with the Hednesford and Cannock Chase District Poultry and Pigeon Society. A few years later the Cannock Flower Show was attracting several thousand to its annual fête. There were probably at least as many keen gardeners a hundred years ago as there are today – the only difference being that vegetable patches, rather than water features, predominated.

All sorts of amateur entertainment flourished. The Hednesford Amateur Minstrels gave regular concerts at the Public Rooms. Then, as now, there were charity events. One special concert was organised for the 'Abercarne Colliery Explosion Fund' in which 270 men and boys were killed. By the early 20th century 'live' entertainment had encountered its first real challenger – the cinema. The Electric Palace at Hednesford, and the Danilo at Cannock were just two of the many cinemas which, between them, entertained thousands of people each week. Bands were a popular form of entertainment and they provided opportunities for

109 Music has a long and proud tradition across the Chase and the area can boast several fine choirs and bands which still exist today. This picture, of the Cheslyn Hay Male Voice Choir in 1948, is just one of many similar groups. Its conductor was Howard Benton, who gave a lifetime of service to music.

110 Cannock Operatic Society. Leading lights included the following names, many of whom are pictured here: May Leek, Bob Wilkes, Gladys Pope, Mary Chackett, Kath Moore, Maud Webster, Frank Yates, Ray Harrison, Betty Jackson, Percy Boot, Dorothy Jones, George Whitehouse, Dolly Linford, Bradford Mansty, Mabel Heath, Blanche Boot, Laurie Taylor and Ruby Lockett.

111 A bonfire to be proud of! This one was erected on the Brotherhood Field, Heath Hayes. A local man, Sam Barber, was the driving force behind the 'Brotherhood' for many years. Similar bonfires seemed to be a feature of the area and were built to mark special events such as King George V's Silver Jubilee in 1935. Imagine the number of gardens that could be 'decked' with all those railway sleepers!

112 Tom Coulthwaite, 'The Wizard of the Turf', in 1939. He gave this signed photograph to 'Mack', his chauffeur, Jim Macpherson. Many local people recall tales of his kindness and generosity.

many people to enjoy music. Both Great Wyrley and Cheslyn Hay had excellent brass bands, as did Cannock. However, the *Cannock Advertiser* was moved to ask 'Are Cannockites music loving?' when, in 1878, the Cannock Brass Band performed on the bowling green each Friday evening to only a handful of people. Things must have picked up in later years when Cannock could boast a bandstand in the park and one in the centre of town, erected at one end of the old bowling green – complete with public toilets underneath!

The railways also transformed leisure and holiday opportunities for local folk. All sorts of organisations were involved. Seven hundred men employed by the West Cannock Colliery Company took a trip to Aston Park and Grounds in 1879, paid for by their Sick and Accident Club. In the same year 401 Wesleyans went to Blackpool for the day. They were followed by 1,500 men and their families from the Cannock and Rugeley Colliery Company who also went to Blackpool by train from Hednesford 'at the trifling charge of 2s. per head'.

The Chase can also lay claim to a long and successful association with all manner of sports. Hednesford Hills was a very important training ground for horses from the 18th to the 20th centuries. In the days before railways, horses were walked to race meetings. Apparently it took a stable lad six days to walk a horse to York. The story of a horse called Independence shows just what this meant. Independence was trained at Hednesford by a well-known trainer named Flintoff. In 1832 Independence walked to Warwick and won two races there. He was then led to Doncaster and won

113 Grakle takes the last jump in the 1931 Grand National and secures Coulthwaite's third victory at Aintree.

two more races. Independence then won another race at Hollywell. Next the horse walked to Chester and won the Chester Cup, and on the way back to Hednesford stopped off to win another race at Manchester.

Many famous trainers and jockeys are associated with the Hednesford Hills training grounds. John Wilkins, keeper of the *Cross Keys Inn*, trained Jealousy, the 1861 Grand National winner. However, Tom Coulthwaite was, undoubtedly, the greatest trainer of all, despite the fact that he never rode a horse himself. He came from Manchester in 1899 and opened his stables at Hazelslade. Years later he moved them to Flaxley Green, near Rugeley. His three Grand National winners are part of the folklore of the Chase. Eremon won in 1907, Jenkinstown in 1910 and Grakle in 1931. It was Grakle's fifth attempt at the Grand National and he won in a record time of 9 minutes 32.8 seconds. Keith Piggot, Lester Piggot's father, should have ridden Grakle but broke a leg and was replaced by Bob Lyall instead. It was a sign of the times that hundreds of Chase enthusiasts were able to follow the breathless commentary on the radio.

Tom Coulthwaite enjoyed many other successes over the years. In 1912 Rathlea brought home three major trophies, the Liverpool Spring Cup, the Great North Handicap at York and the Chester Cup. Coulthwaite's magic touch extended to 'no hopers' as well. Salmon Fly was sent to Coulthwaite as a last resort when no buyer could be found for him, but the 'Wizard' astounded the racing world when Salmon Fly won four important races, one

114 Hednesford Town FC. The 1910 Birmingham Combination champions. Back row: Gough, Reaney, Picken, Greenway, Mobberley and Corbett. Front row: Bristow, Jukes, Sheldon, Cumberlidge and Lloyd.

115 The Bourne Methodist Tennis Club, Heath Hayes, *c*.1905.

116 Salem Football Club, Cheslyn Hay, 1926-7 season. Just one of many local amateur teams who played in the district. Back row: W. Bull, H. Perks, T. Hawkins, S. Smith, H. Brough, A. Hood, D. Hood, E. Sambooks, H. Harvey, W. Goodman, B. Plant, -?-. Front row: B. Brough, R. Hawkins, F. Richards, S. Perry, -?-, E. Smith. Sitting: R. Fletcher and J. Shorter.

after the other, winning a total of £4,300. Such was his phenomenal success that tongues began to wag. Allegations were made against Coulthwaite that he doped his winners, and he had his licence suspended in 1913 by the National Hunt Committee. Coulthwaite strenuously protested his innocence but he did not get his licence back until after the First World War. Happily he went on to achieve one of his greatest wins with Grakle in 1931.

There have also been some proud moments in football and Hednesford Town Football Club has made sporting headlines more than once. The club was formed in 1880 when two local teams combined and based themselves at the *Anglesey Hotel*. In 1887, the year before the formation of the Football League, Aston Villa played against Hednesford at the Anglesey ground for a 'Benefit Match for Hednesford Town'. Hednesford were four goals down at half-time but played well in the second half for a final score of 4-3. In 1904 the club moved to the *Cross Keys*. Many famous players began with Hednesford over the years. Enthusiasts will recognise names such as Jack Devey, Steve Smith and Orlando Evans who all went on to play for Aston Villa. Charlie Crossley went on to play for Walsall, then Sunderland and Everton. The great Billy Walker played for Hednesford for one season in 1911 before moving to Villa. He played for England 13 times and was later a successful manager of both Sheffield Wednesday and then Nottingham Forest. Jack 'Tosh' Evans helped take Hednesford through successful seasons in 1912-14 and went on to play

117 Cannock Town FC, 1925-6. The club was one of the casualties of the long depression in the 1930s. Its dilapidated pitch and facilities, known as Brookfields, lay just off the Walsall Road, Cannock. It folded in 1937, despite raising its gate price from 6d. to one shilling.

118 St Chad's School football team, 1938-9. Chadsmoor lads enjoyed a fearsome reputation on the soccer field for many years. They reached their zenith when David Gardiner, the new headmaster of Central Boys' School, nearby, coached the school team in the late 1940s.

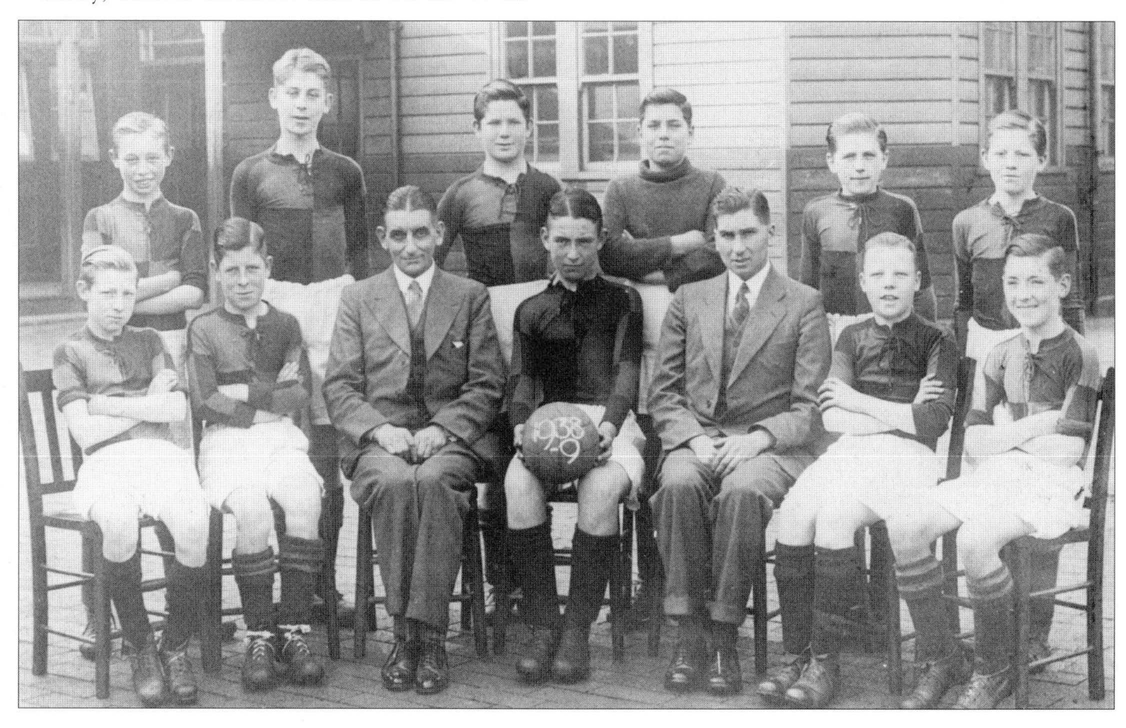

for Wolves. Teddy Bowen and Alec Talbot went to Aston Villa in 1923 and Bob Finch to West Bromwich Albion in 1925. If only Hednesford could have afforded to keep such players!

The nadir for the club was in 1937-8. Funds were so low that the team could not even afford to pay the £20 costs of travelling to Oswestry. The club had to resign from the Birmingham League in February 1938. They were not alone, Cannock Town having already been forced to do the same. But, unlike Cannock, Hednesford rose from the ashes. A new club, Hednesford FC, was formed the following season and continued to play at the *Cross Keys*. The club rejoined the Birmingham League in 1953/4. The remarkable match against premiership side Middlesbrough, in the fourth round of the FA Cup in January 1997, when Hednesford scored the first goal and so nearly pulled off a remarkable win, has already become another piece of the sporting history of the Chase.

119 Boys from Chadsmoor Central School in 1947. They had gone on a week's educational visit to Swanage with their teacher Mr. George Wright. The trip was arranged by the Cannock Rotary Club. The highlight of the week was beating a local football team 7-1.

120 The reservoir, Hednesford Hills. The reservoir was a short-lived venture, following the collapse of part of the bank not long after its completion. It is now the site of Hednesford Hills Raceway.

There have also been countless amateur teams playing over the years, representing church and chapel, workplace or pub. They are too numerous to mention individually. Suffice to say that the team photographs reproduced on these pages each have a story to tell: stories of victories snatched from the jaws of defeat; stories of skilful players who finished their Saturday shift down the pit at two and were playing a match by four; stories of rivalry and friendship, team spirit and proud moments.

121 Mr. Jack Morris enjoyed a long association with Cannock Cricket and Hockey Clubs. Sadly, Mr. Morris died in 1954, just before the clubs' first grounds, in Hatherton Road, were completed. The grounds were rented from Mr. Morris's sister, Mrs. Best, who later sold the site to the club.

122 The youth team of Cannock Cricket and Hockey Clubs, 1912. Back row: A.L. Linford, R. Sellman, R. Evans. Second row: L. Marshall, R. Battersby, C. Lockley. Front row: E. Boot, E. Whitehouse, E.V. Linford, H. Stevens, F. Parsons.

123 A rare picture of part of the demolition of the old Cannock Brewery premises situated off Mill Street, Cannock.

124 Church Hill Victoria Working Men's Club, Hednesford. Working men's clubs were once a familiar sight around the district but they are now declining rapidly – rendered redundant by affluence and changing attitudes towards leisure activities. Nevertheless, in their heyday, these clubs were an important part of every local community. They provided comfortable surroundings, lively entertainment and very good value.

125 The Wimblebury Community Centre football team of 1942-3. As with the working men's club, local community centres were also an important part of local life – from sewing clubs to beetle drives, as well as many sporting activities.

126 The Old Brindley Village Club, *c.*1950. A Football and Darts Presentation evening. Surnames include: Whitehouse, Leadbeater, Jones, Heathcote, Dyas, Parsons, Pickles, Westwood, Ford, Waltho, Kirkham, Crowder, Lyons, Evans, Clare, Denny, Hawthorn, Bullock, Mason, Smith, Crutchley, Dando, Williams, Craddock, Mills, Felton, Oats, McGuire and Duffy. Such clubs were a vital part of each community - much more than just a place to drink.

The Cannock Hockey and Cricket Clubs are now into their third century and are going from strength to strength. Today the hockey club can boast Olympic-class players, and the facilities at Hatherton are some of the best in the country. This success is largely due to a combination of enthusiasm, hard work, sportsmanship and the generosity of people who have enjoyed, in some cases, a lifetime's association with the clubs. Jack Morris and his sister, Mrs. Best, enabled the clubs to have their first permanent grounds in Hatherton Road. In doing so they gave the clubs a secure financial future second to none.

Football, cricket and hockey are just three of the many sports which have been played and enjoyed in the district. Rugby, tennis, badminton, pigeon racing, dog racing, the raceway, fishing, bowls, athletics and swimming enthusiasts also have their place in history. It is fitting to end this chapter with a mention of one of Cannock's oldest sports, bowling. The town can boast an ancient bowling green which dates back to the time when the green was enclosed by a wall back in 1752-3, and it is highly likely that bowls were played on the green long before then. Somehow the green has survived to see in the 21st century – a picturesque reminder of times past, and long may it remain so.

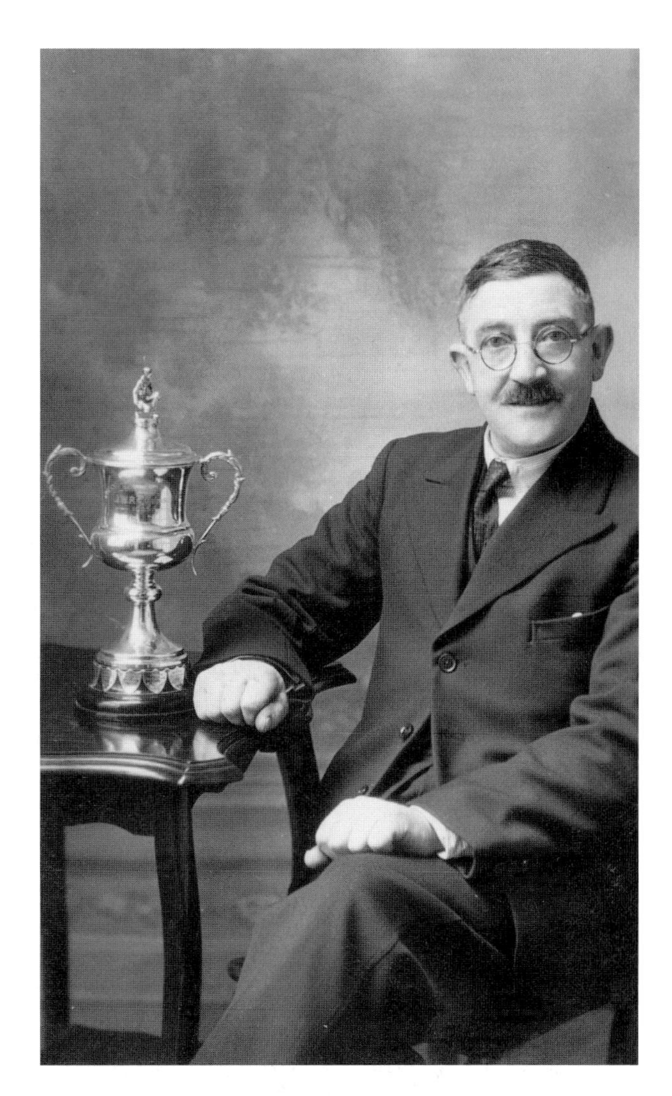

127 Mr. Tom Cooper, for many years a carpenter at Hawkins' Colliery. He is pictured with the Woodman Bowling Cup, *c.*1930. At that time bowling was a very popular and competitive pastime. Many local public houses across the district boasted a fine bowling green until well into the 1950s.

Twelve

Victims and Villains

Where crime is concerned it is a fallacy to think that things are much worse today. Memories of more law-abiding decades such as the 1930s and 1950s, still fresh in the minds of many, tend to give a false impression. In fact, far longer periods in the past have been lawless and violent. Delve back into local records and every sort of crime is there – from shoplifting to murder. Notorious cases are part of the folklore of the Chase. 'Palmer the poisoner' and the 'Wyrley Gang' have been turned into television and radio dramas. And 'Gaskin's Wood' has featured in Halloween events which re-enact the gruesome murder and dismemberment of Elizabeth, by her estranged husband, Thomas Gaskin. For different reasons, in all three cases, the convictions which followed were 'dodgy', to say the least.

William Palmer lived at Rugeley but his fascination with horse racing often saw him at Hednesford. In 1851 there were 120 blood horses stabled and trained in the district. Indirectly, they led to Palmer's undoing. Palmer seems to have been a thoroughly bad lot from an early age. His infamous career of crime only lasted so long because

128 Cannock town centre in the early 1950s – quiet, respectable and much more law abiding!

129 The grave of 'Palmer the Poisoner' at Stafford Gaol. Palmer was hanged in front of a crowd of, reputedly, some thirty thousand people! Many had travelled long distances – made possible by the advent of the railways.

he was such a plausible charmer. By the time he became a doctor in Rugeley he had squandered his inheritance and reckless gambling was already a way of life. Within a few years his medical practice in Rugeley had virtually ceased.

He had probably murdered at least three people, including his mother-in-law, by then. That was May 1850. Other suspicious deaths followed in quick succession. Palmer's main motive was greed. He killed either to save money or obtain money. He disposed of encumbrances such as his children, born to both his wife and his mistress, Eliza Tharm. He also killed people for their life insurance. He received £13,000 when his wife died, supposedly of 'English Cholera'. However, the company refused to pay another £14,000 on the death of his brother, Walter, a few months later. Foolishly, he ignored the warning signs and his crimes became more reckless. The last of his victims was J. Parsons Cook, who died in November 1855. It is believed that Parsons died of strychnine poisoning. Gossip and rumour crystallised into open accusations and Palmer was arrested. He was convicted at the Old Bailey but was brought back to Stafford Gaol to be hanged before a crowd of 30,000, in June 1856. Few people doubted that Palmer was a serial killer, but the validity of his conviction was hotly debated at the time. Forensic tests, such as they were, failed to identify the poison used. It was Palmer's reputation which placed the noose around his neck.

Such was Rugeley's notoriety that it is said the town petitioned the Prime Minister, Palmerston, for permission to change its name. Apparently he consented, on condition that the town was named after himself. Not surprisingly the idea was dropped.

130 George Edalji. He was wrongly convicted of the early animal maimings at Great Wyrley. Mr Edalji was sentenced to seven years' penal servitude in October 1903. He was released three years later and finally granted a free pardon in May 1907.

131 Members of the Hickman family of Station Street, Cheslyn Hay. Sisters Florrie Cooper and Rachel Harvey stand behind their mother, Mrs. Hickman. Their cousin Daisy Weller (left) and sister Jane Hughes stand either side of Mrs. Hickman. Beatrice Holland is seated holding her son George. Their father was an overman at The Nook colliery. Respectable local people such as these were, no doubt, horrified by the actions of 'The Wyrley Gang'.

The 'Wyrley Gang' animal maimings and the conviction of George Edalji is another case of a very dubious conviction. In 1903 nine animals were killed or mutilated in Cheslyn Hay and Great Wyrley. Suspicion fell on George Edalji. In hindsight, he was a very unlikely suspect. His father, born in Bombay, became a Christian and attended a theological college at Canterbury. Following his ordination he married an English lady and, thanks to his wife's influence, he became vicar of St Mark's, Great Wyrley. The family encountered prejudice, suspicion and harassment over the years, which culminated in the conviction of the eldest son, George Edalji, a Birmingham solicitor.

The police handling of the case is not to their credit. The investigation appears not to have been impartial, thorough or reliable. Looking back it seems as if Edalji's guilt was assumed and the prosecution was selective, to say the least, with the evidence presented at the trial. His father campaigned for George's release and many eminent people expressed doubts about the conviction, including Sir Arthur Conan Doyle. Doyle went so far as to visit Great Wyrley and his investigations led him to accuse another local man, Royden Smith, instead. Edalji was released from jail in October 1906 and given a free pardon – but no compensation – in May 1907. However, the Law Society had no

headquarters market place wyrley
warning notice
that man who was seen early on
thursday morning in a field is the same
man who done the maiming outrage
at walsall early on friday morning
I paid him well to do the outrage
but if that man gave him up to
the police on thursday morning he
would have been a dead man before
long, signed g h darby captain of
the wyrley gang.

132 One of many letters written by 'g h darby captain of the wyrley gang'. Captain Darby was the alias of Enoch Knowles, who was finally convicted of sending hundreds of malicious letters to various people in October 1934.

qualms about his character and reinstated Edalji. He quietly picked up the pieces of his life and lived until 1953.

So, what is the connection between Edalji and the Wyrley Gang? Other outrages occurred in 1907, 1912, 1913 and 1915. There were at least two perpetrators. Local miner Thomas Farrington was convicted of maiming two sheep and a lamb in 1904, a case of a drunk committing a copycat crime. Some of the other crimes may have been of a similar nature. What is certain is that there was no 'Wyrley Gang'; in fact the 'Wyrley Gang' was a red herring and the figment of a thoroughly nasty imagination. But that does not stop dozens of elderly residents over the age of 80 claiming to know the identity of at least one member of the gang! Such are the pitfalls of local history.

The Wyrley Gang association was begun in October 1903 by a poorly written note sent by 'g.h.darby, captain of the wyrley gang' threatening further killings and pouring scorn on the police.

I have known Mr. James H
Rogers for more than fifteen years,
and am able to certify from personal
knowledge that he is a person of
good character, is steady, sober
and honest, and can be relied upon
to manage any business he undertakes
with care, diligence and faithfulness.
S Edalji
Vicar of Great Wyrley.

9th. Nov. 1909.

133 A reference from George Edalji's father, the vicar of Great Wyrley, dated 9 November 1909. By then George had been released. The letter suggests that the prejudice and hostility the Edaljis endured was less widespread than might be supposed. The Rogers family kept the *Woodman Inn* at Cheslyn Hay at the time, and a local licensee's views would have counted for a lot. Other family papers show that there had been connections between the two families for many years.

Feb 20

Mrs Talbot

Lizzie is quite alright she is with me now I met her at Hednesford on Thursday she was crying, she told me her husband was making a fool of her, so I told her to leave all and come with me she will send you some money when we get to London, we are going there next week she will write herself when when we get there, she is very upset now I can asure you she will be alright with me hoping you dont mind

From Lizzies Friend
W. Brooks

134 Famous last words! A note from Lizzie Gaskin's lover, written just a few days before her murder.

Further letters and postcards followed intermittently between 1907 and 1923. Some accurately predicted attacks on animals; no wonder many believed that the 'Wyrley Gang' existed. Then years later, in 1934, the culprit was caught thanks to a sharp-eyed Black Country postmistress who recognised the handwriting. G.H. Darby turned out to be Enoch Knowles of Darlaston. Over a period of thirty years Knowles had sent hundreds of threatening and abusive letters to many different people, often those connected with serious crimes reported in the press. Knowles had escaped detection because he pretended to be illiterate. He was jailed for three years.

The third notorious case was the murder of Elizabeth Gaskin in 1919. Her husband confessed when he was arrested, was convicted and hanged at Winson Green in Birmingham the following July. It was a horrible crime but were there mitigating circumstances? His wife had had two illegitimate children whilst he was in the army during the First World War, which, according to his confession, preyed on his mind. Although they lived apart on

135 One of several postcards published following the murder of Lizzie Gaskin. The gasometer, where Gaskin dumped his wife's body, was situated in Victoria Street, Hednesford.

his return, Gaskin pestered his wife so much that she planned to move to Birmingham. Instead, after another stormy encounter, she was brutally killed in the woods near to what is now the Museum of Cannock Chase.

He was judged to be sane and fit to stand trial. Dr. Butter, of Cannock, stated, 'He was *compos mentis* when he committed the deed. He had a very clear memory of the facts 4 days later.' Later, on 19 April, one W. Cassels, a Medical Officer, reported, 'Prisoner has been under my observation here since his reception and I have had frequent conversations with him. I have not observed any unsoundness of mind.' Nevertheless, who is to say that he was not affected by the horrors of fighting in the First World War? And what of local recollections of Gaskin riding through Hednesford and discharging a shotgun on more than one occasion? Modern psychiatrists would probably have saved Gaskin from the gallows.

Very few local females have been convicted of murder. Sarah Westwood of Burntwood is an

136 The *Star* public house at Burntwood. The inquest into the death of Sarah Westwood's husband was held at the *Star* where a verdict of murder was returned. Sarah was convicted of poisoning him with arsenic. There was no reliable forensic test to establish such poisoning in 1843. Nevertheless, a bad reputation and gossip was enough to condemn her!

137 Samson Blewitt standing behind his dog. This picture was taken some thirty years after the shooting incident which led to the conviction of two local men.

unfortunate exception. Curiously, her case has been virtually forgotten. Sarah was executed in 1844 for supposedly poisoning her husband with arsenic, served in a bowl of gruel. She too was hanged in front of a large crowd at Stafford Gaol. Like Palmer, Sarah Westwood's reputation was her undoing, rather than sound forensic evidence. She was born in Chorley in 1817. Her family moved to Burntwood when her father, Charles Parker, had the opportunity to build his own cottage. Sarah had an illegitimate daughter 18 months before she married, which tainted her character. She was married for twenty years and the couple had seven children aged between 19 and five. Judging by the couple's public and very heated arguments it was a stormy marriage, and witnesses reported hearing Sarah wish her husband dead. He died soon afterwards, apparently poisoned. The inquest was held at the old *Star Inn* at Burntwood and caused a lot of morbid interest. When it emerged that she had obtained arsenic from a Walsall chemist, and gossips suggested that the family's lodger, Samuel Phillips was her lover, her fate was sealed. Sarah was sent for trial. She died, in front of a large crowd, protesting her innocence to the last.

Perhaps it would have been better for both of them if Sarah's husband had sold her at a market. Another Burntwood man did just that in 1837: George Hitchinson took his wife, Elizabeth, to Walsall market with a halter fastened around her neck. One Thomas Snape, a Burntwood nailer, purchased her for 2s. 6d. Apparently Elizabeth and Thomas were already living together. In those days a public sale was quicker and cheaper than a divorce. Reading between the lines, it would seem that women were only permitted to give their husbands away.

The years between Palmer and Gaskin saw the total transformation of the economy of the Chase. As a result the social order was turned upside down. For fifty or so years old ways sat uneasily alongside the new. And as the population increased so did crime, which rarely made national news. In January 1884 the Reverend Bullivant of Hednesford was shot at during the day whilst walking between Hill Top and East Cannock. Luckily the bullet only hit his hat, but no one was apprehended. However, this was not a major story; the incident merely featured in a letter of complaint by Bullivant himself. In February 1900 Pye Green farmer, Samson Blewitt, challenged two poachers on his farm and was shot and seriously wounded. Undeterred, he 'bravely followed' the pair and was threatened again. Fortunately, he managed to get to Hednesford police station. His assailants, brothers George and John Jenkinson, were arrested soon afterwards and charged with GBH. Samson Blewitt survived; Harry Cook, a police constable based at Hednesford, was not so fortunate. He 'died in the course of his duty' in 1879 when he tackled poachers. His tombstone

138 A rare view of Wyrley and Cheslyn Hay station. This pleasant, orderly scene, possibly folk waiting for an excursion train, belies its reputation as a haunt for 'large numbers of youths who infest Wyrley Station' back in the 1880s. Virtually nothing of the site remains, although the railway line re-opened to passenger traffic some years ago.

can still be seen in the churchyard at St Peter's, Hednesford.

Complaints about 'large numbers of youths who infest Wyrley Station' and whose language is 'beastly' sounds all too modern. However, the great-great-grandfathers of today's youth were making a thorough nuisance of themselves back in 1884. Their behaviour was so bad that it intimidated, even terrified, local residents. Calls for a stronger police presence fell on deaf ears. A familiar sound! Drunkenness brought many problems too. Letters to local newspapers regularly complained about damage to property, bad language, rudeness and fighting. Stella Orme, who lived in Bradbury Lane at her parents' shop in the 1920s, clearly recalls that local constables would only venture there on Saturday nights in twos or threes. Forty years before, in the 1880s, the Chief Constable of Staffordshire invented a 'light wicker shield' for constables to carry on their backs at night because of the risks they took 'in encounters with the rougher elements of a mining and agricultural district'.

The arrival of the railway was a boon to enterprising criminals. Today they use the motorway network but trains were used in much the same way by the 1870s. There are quite a few reports of Black Country thieves travelling to the Chase. For example, Martin Flannagan of Brierley Hill and John Hill of Dudley were convicted of shoplifting in Cannock and Wyrley in 1878.

Reports of female crime were far fewer. One which stands out is coal stealing, especially during depressions or strikes. The usual defence was poverty. These women were mostly caught picking over the colliery waste heaps. They were usually fined but, as in the case of three women who stole

139 Coal pickers at the Wimblebury colliery, during a strike in the early 1920s. A blind eye was often turned when severe hardship forced mining families to scavenge for coal on colliery heaps. But this was not always the case and there are many examples of successful prosecutions, which sometimes resulted in jail sentences – even for women.

160lb. of coal from the West Cannock Colliery Company, they sometimes received prison sentences of seven or fourteen days.

Cruelty to children and animals provoked outrage then, as now. There are some particularly awful reports of cruelty to pit ponies when underground. Contemporary sources often give the impression that such behaviour was only to be expected from miners. In December 1890, John Harley, a miner, of Rawnsley was charged with cruelty to his children, according to the *Cannock Advertiser*. This provoked an irate response from J. Baker of Five Ways, whose letter read, 'Now this is a mistake and will you please to correct it … for Harley is not a miner but a boiler worker. I do not mean to say that the miners are free from blame in every respect, but I do say that they are too often made the scape goat to bear the sins of others.'

Infringements of game laws often carried heavier penalties than other crimes. Charles Wood from Cheslyn Hay was fined £2 with £1 2s. 6d. costs for shooting a hare in 1878. A year later a Chadsmoor man was fined 10s. for taking a partridge from a trap. Compare this to the fine of 10s. for a violent assault on a miner working at the Cannock and Rugeley No.1 pit around the same time. Here we can see a local example of the uneasy transition from a traditional rural society into an industrial one. In the main local JPs were the principal landowners and the likes of Lord Hatherton no doubt had strong views about poachers.

The Industrial Revolution transformed society in its working practices too. Inhumanely long working weeks, no effective safety legislation and no concept of employers' liability stacked the odds against employees. Workers had very few rights in the 19th century; they even faced prosecution if they broke company rules. In 1882 a group of miners from Five Ways were found 'unlawfully sleeping in a fire hole' at the West Cannock Colliery No.1 pit at 1a.m. They received a sentence of seven days' hard labour! A week before two Mid-Cannock miners were each fined five shillings for leaving their employment without giving notice. A collier at the Cannock and Leacroft Colliery was fined 20s. with 13s. 6d. costs when he was found to be in breach of safety rules after he refused a manager's order to place a 'cog' to support the longwall face he was working. The miner's defence was that no support was needed as no fault was present. He was fined nonetheless. A few years later two miners working for the East Cannock Colliery Company were fined around 9s. at the petty sessions for refusing to work on after a roof fall, a case of damned if you do and damned if you don't!

The Liberal reforms in the early part of the 20th century marked the beginning of the end of such iniquities. The First World War and its aftermath also hastened change. Hardly anyone was left who could remember a time before 'coal was king'. A golden age of community policing and trust in the law was dawning and it coincided with the lifetime of Cannock's new police station, opened in 1923. It was based at the former home of the famous Dr. Butter, and stood at the corner of Victoria Street and Wolverhampton Road. It was one of the many lovely buildings which once graced Cannock. Sadly, it did not meet the needs of modern policing and was replaced by the present station in 1968. Its demolition coincided with the end of the 'Heartbeat' years of policing, when everything seemed in its right place. What we have now feels far less reassuring.

140 Miners are one of the most stereotyped groups of workers ever to have existed. Broad and damning generalisations hide the fact that many were respectable, hard-working men. Mr. Lycett, of Littleworth, dressed in his mine's rescue gear, typifies the other side of the case.

Thirteen

The Arsenal of England

The Chase might have had a very different history if it had become the arsenal of England. Detailed proposals were under active consideration, around 1860, to move the arsenal from Woolwich. Part of the Chase appeared to meet the criteria. An advert in a Walsall newspaper in July 1860 offered building land for sale, situated between the *Uxbridge Arms* (Chasetown) and Burntwood that was 'within half a mile of the proposed site for the government arsenal'. The central location, cheap land, canal and rail links, and a plentiful supply of coal for the munitions factories made the Chase an ideal place in the minds of Victorian civil servants.

Perhaps J.R. McClean had had a hand in the plans? He was an influential civil engineer with London connections. Furthermore, McClean had various business interests on the Chase, including the Cannock Chase Colliery Company. In addition, he already owned a lot of freehold land in the area; and he was heavily involved in the building of two local railways to ensure the best markets for his coal. Such an able engineer, and a typical Victorian entrepreneur to boot, must have realised the potential of the re-location of the national arsenal alongside his mines. Fortunately, the scheme never materialised – just imagine the bombing raids which would have taken place during the Second World War had the arsenal been located here.

This was not the only time that the War Office focused on the Chase. The great Autumn Manoeuvres of 1873 brought several thousand regular soldiers to 12 camping grounds, each carefully surveyed beforehand. Rawnsley Hills, Brindley Heath, Sherbrook Pools and Hednesford Hills were four of the sites provided for cavalry, artillery and infantry units. Surviving notes about the camping grounds indicate that army surveyors were looking for well-drained land with good quality water supplies. Brindley Heath apparently had an unlimited supply of good drinking water from streams and pools, and the same was true for Sherbrook. At the Hednesford Hills site, Hednesford Pool was deemed fit for drinking but not the Bentley Brook. At that time the pool was partly fed by 'very good water flowing in a culvert from the colliery' (the Valley). Hednesford railway also fitted the bill as it was 'well suited to the arrival and departure of troops, with good sidings and field close by for stores'. Just this one site on the Hednesford Hills provided the army with 191 acres of training ground; no wonder the local people talked about the manoeuvres for years afterwards.

There were further military manoeuvres in 1894, but not on such a grand scale, and volunteer battalions, usually local ones, often used the area, especially around Teddesley Park. Things quietened down for a while – the Boer Wars did away with the need for such manoeuvres – but it was not to last and the War Office was back with a vengeance in 1914. The First World War had a huge impact on the area. Two sprawling army training camps, Rugeley Camp and Brocton Camp, covered vast tracts of the Chase. The camps were separated by the Sherbrook Valley. Denuded of trees, the landscape must have presented a cheerless, desolate face to the estimated quarter of a million or so people (the Women's Auxiliary Army Corps also trained at Brocton) who passed through the camps. Similar transit or training camps were erected all over England, but the Chase camps were some of the largest.

Over a million men had enlisted by the end of 1914 but the permanent barracks could accommodate only 175,000 troops. Urgent action

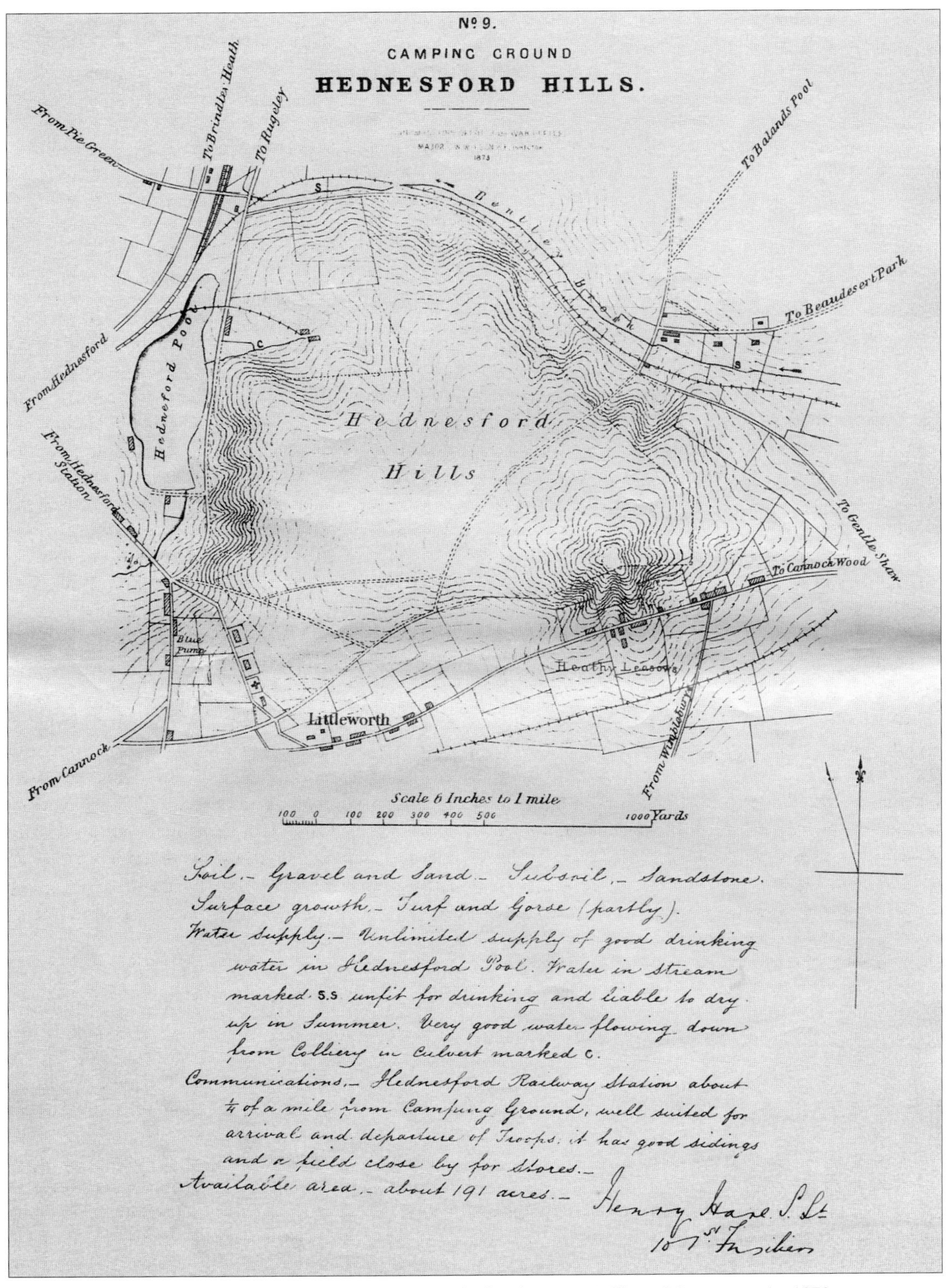

No 9.
CAMPING GROUND
HEDNESFORD HILLS.
From Pie Green
To Brindley Heath
To Rugeley
To Balands Pool
Bentley Brook
To Beaudesert Park
From Hednesford
Hednesford Pool
Hednesford Hills
From Hednesford Station
To Gentle Shaw
To Cannock Wood
Blue Pump
Heathy Leasows
Littleworth
From Cannock
From Wimblebury
Scale 6 Inches to 1 mile
100 0 100 200 300 400 500 1000 Yards
Soil.– Gravel and Sand.– Subsoil.– Sandstone.
Surface growth.– Turf and Gorse (partly).
Water supply.– Unlimited supply of good drinking water in Hednesford Pool. Water in Stream marked S.S unfit for drinking and liable to dry up in Summer. Very good water flowing down from Colliery in Culvert marked C.
Communications.– Hednesford Railway Station about ¼ of a mile from Camping Ground, well suited for arrival and departure of Troops. it has good sidings and a field close by for Stores.–
Available area.– about 191 acres.–
Henry Hare S. Lt
101st Fusiliers

141 The survey of Hednesford Hills made for the great Military Manoeuvres in 1873.

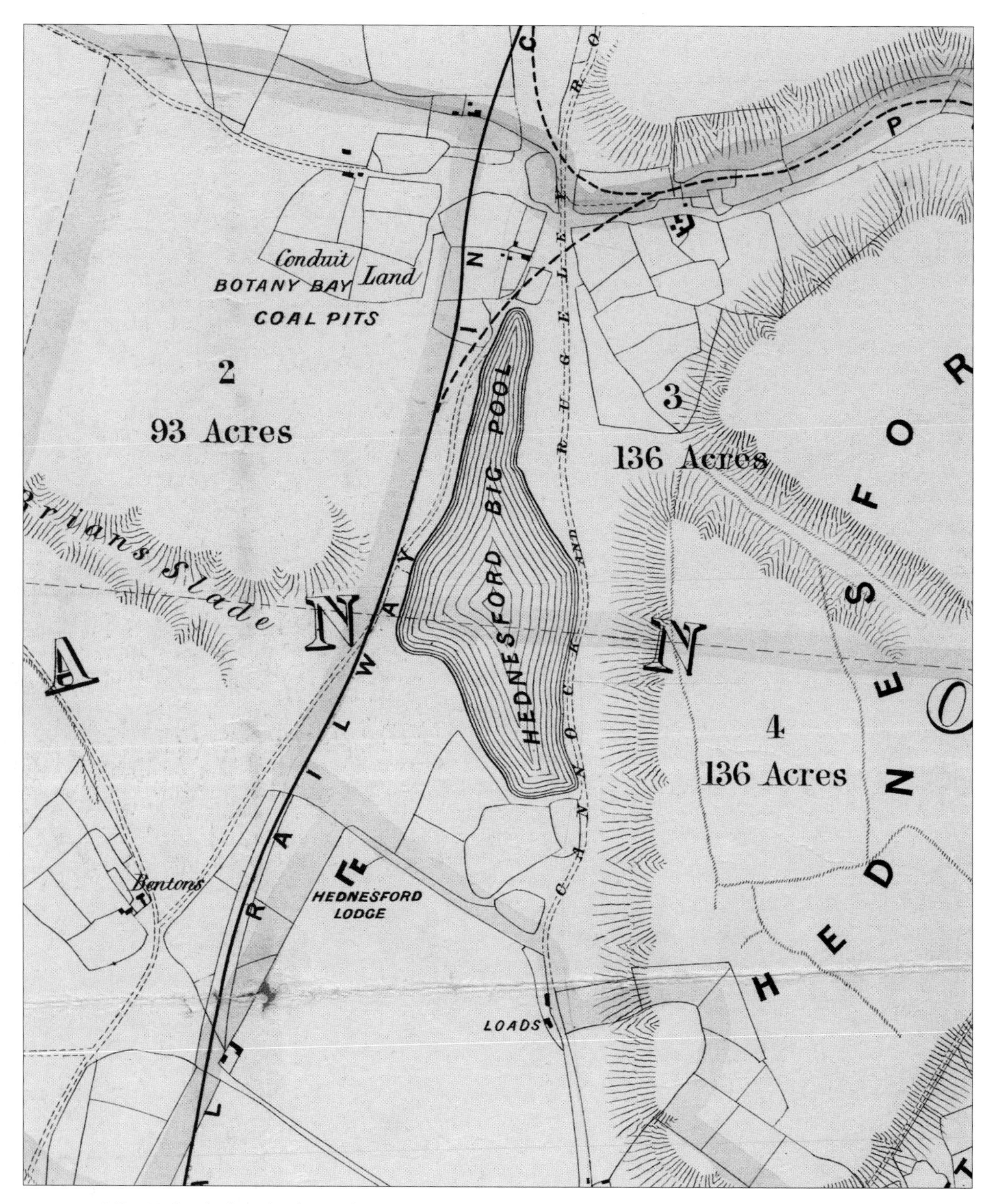

142 Hednesford Pool. The pool must have been a very attractive feature of the area. It also provided drinking water and was well stocked with fish. However, as the new town grew so did the problem of flooding and the pool was eventually drained. Part of the pool is now the site of Hednesford Park.

143 Anson Bank Camp, Brocton. Traces of the camp can still be seen, located between the Katyn memorial and the Glacial Boulder.

was required. Patriotic feeling ran high and local landowners such as Lord Lichfield and the Marquis of Anglesey made land available. A basic infrastructure for the camps was in place by the middle of 1915. Roads and rail track had been laid, along with power, fuel and water supplies. The provision of standard gauge railway tracks became the responsibility of the West Cannock Colliery Company, and it was then that the well-known 'Tackeroo' line was constructed. Water was pumped from Sherbrook Valley until boreholes were sunk nearer the camps. Rows and rows of wooden huts, smelling of creosote in the summer and coke stoves and damp in the winter, dominated the landscape. Both camps were self-contained communities by 1917. Basic amenities such as YMCA canteens, church huts, post offices and banks, even a book stall run by W.H. Smith and Son, helped to make life a little less bleak.

At first they were only transit camps, a staging post before Front Line service. But as more and more raw recruits joined, Brocton and Rugeley became training camps, complete with ranges, instead. Many recruits were not only raw but very young. My grandfather was wounded in the First Battle of the Somme before he was seventeen. Many other families can tell a similar tale. Such actions reflect very different attitudes; a time, for example, when patriotic pride was valued rather than ridiculed.

In the autumn of 1917 there were around 1,500,000 British forces and 200,000 Dominion troops in training camps across the UK. A large contingent of New Zealanders was based on the Chase, and known affectionately as 'The Dinks'.

144 General view of the Army Camps of Cannock Chase during the First World War. The picture does not really convey how bleak the camps seemed to most of the soldiers.

145 Hednesford's first taxi service, owned by Mr. Shaw, seated in the front taxi. Walter Harvey is driving the other car and George Turner can be seen standing. The Brindley Heath Hospital is in the background. The taxi service prospered because of the remote location of the Chase camps.

Freda and Snooks are two more names associated with the New Zealanders. The grave of Freda, a Dalmatian bitch and popular regimental mascot of the New Zealand Rifle Brigade, can still be seen today. The cookhouse cat, Snooks, was probably the best fed animal in Staffordshire at the time.

Towards the end of the war German POWs lived in a separate part of Brocton Camp. They worked on farms and building projects in the vicinity with minimal security. This caused some disquiet as it was felt that they received much better treatment than Allied POWs in Germany. Apparently the remains of an escape tunnel was discovered after the war, although no successful escapes were reported. The gravelly soil must have been the very devil to shore up. Subsequent quarrying for gravel has destroyed a large part of the Brocton site. Curiosities such as a scale model of

Rugeley Camp.

THERE'S an isolated, desolated spot I'd like to mention,
Where all you hear is "Stand at Ease," "Slope Arms,
"Quick March," "Attention,"
It's miles away from anywhere, by Gad, it is a rum'un,
A chap lived there for fifty years and never saw a woman.

There's only two lamps in the place, so tell it to your mother,
The postman carries one, and the policeman has the other,
And if you want a jolly night, and do not care a jot,
You take a ride upon the car, the car they haven't got.

There are lots of little huts, all dotted here and there,
For those who have to live inside, I've offered many a prayer
Inside the huts, there's RATS as big as any Nanny Goat,
Last night a soldier saw One Fitting on his Overcoat.

For Breakfast every morning, just like Old Mother Hubbard,
You Double round the bloomin' Hut and jump up at the cupboard
Sometimes you get bacon, and sometimes "lively" cheese,
That forms Platoon upon your plate, Orders Arms and Stands
at Ease.

It's mud up to the eyebrows, you get it in your ears,
But into it you've got to go without a sign of fear,
And when you've had a bath of dust, you just set to and groom,
And get cleaned up for next Parade, or else it's "Orderly Room,

Week in, week out, from morn till night, with full Pack and a rifle,
Like Jack and Jill, you climb the hills, of course that's just a trifle,
"Slope Arms," "Fix Bayonets," then "Present" they fairly put
you through it.
And as you stagger to your hut, the Sergeant shouts "Jump to it,

There's another kind of drill, especially invented for the Army,
I think they call it Swedish, and it nearly drives you barmy;
This blinking drill it does you good, it makes your bones so tender
You can coil yourself up like a snake and crawl beneath the fender.

With tunics, boots and putties off, you quickly get the habit,
You gallop up and down the hills just like a blooming rabbit,
"Heads Backward Bend," "Arms Upward Stretch," "Heels
Raise," then "Ranks Change Places,"
And later on they make you put your kneecaps where your face is,

Now when this War is over and we've captured Kaiser Billy,
To shoot him would be merciful and absolutely silly,
Just send him down to our little lot, among the rats and clay,
And I'll bet it won't be long before he droops and fades away.

BUT WE'RE STILL "MERRY AND BRIGHT."

From Will.

146 A heartfelt account of life at the Rugeley Camp during the First World War.
It is to be hoped the 'Will' survived.

147 George Vernon Grainger, wounded at the Second Battle of the Somme on 4 October 1916, before he was seventeen. Having lost the use of his left arm he had limited opportunities for work. Nevertheless, he ran a successful lending library from a stall in Cannock Market for some years and he was also a relieving officer in the district during the 1926 Miners' Strike.

Messines Ridge (probably built by German POWs) have all but disappeared. The model may have been constructed for instructional purposes, to demonstrate to troops the art of a 'perfect attack' – a rare event in that terrible war.

Some of the soldiers made an unexpected return visit to the Chase as patients at Brindley Heath military hospital. Twelve separate wards were linked by a main corridor. Other huts provided accommodation for the medical staff. Again, the West Cannock Colliery Company helped out by providing electricity. Unlike the other camps, it remained in full use after the war as the Brindley Heath Ministry of Pensions Hospital. Later still it became a miners' village complete with a school. There was a tremendous community spirit about this village which lived on long after it was demolished in the 1950s.

A handwritten account of life in Hednesford in the early years of the 20th century by William Sharman provides some wonderful descriptions of the times. He was still at school when the war started and he recalls watching the camps being built. His mother took in washing for some of the

soldiers and William had the job of collecting and returning the laundry. William made friends with one of the soldiers who worked in a cookhouse, and he was allowed to collect scraps of food at night for the family's pig. This was illegal and once he was nearly caught by redcaps and only escaped because he knew the Chase so well. By the time he reached home William was more upset at having been forced to dump the food than anything else. William also recalled another soldier saying he had returned to his hut one night to find a rat trying on his greatcoat. Apparently, the

148 Joe Dutton of Great Wyrley worked at Gilpin's and like many other lads enlisted well before his eighteenth birthday – stung by the bitter reproach of a bereaved workmate whose son had been killed. Joe was badly wounded and died shortly before the end of the war.

149 The road leading to the Ministry of Pensions Hospital, Brindley Heath, *c.*1920. A much more pleasant view than the regimented pine tree plantations which have since been planted in the vicinity.

150 The 'Sisters' Quarters' at the Ministry of Pensions Hospital at Brindley Heath, Cannock Chase. These huts also provided homes for the doctors and their families after the war.

camps were infested with huge rats, which caused all sorts of problems.

The 'German Cemetery' is nowadays the only permanent reminder of the camps. It was constructed on land given by the Earl of Lichfield. Older people still refer to it as the 'German Cemetery' even though most of those buried there were New Zealanders, victims of the 1918 'flu epidemic. The true German Cemetery was created in the 1960s, on land nearby, when almost all German military personnel killed in action in and around Britain were reburied on the Chase. By the early 1920s nature had begun to reclaim the abandoned parts of the camps. Most of the huts were sold off. Several went to Brocton village. Another became a Scout hut at Bloxwich. Others ended up as homes situated along the A34 at Great Wyrley that were only demolished in 1968. No doubt many other bits and pieces found their way into local homes and gardens. Finally, new Forestry Commission plantations gradually swallowed up the remains.

The Second World War also left its mark. Changing methods of warfare meant that the Royal Air Force needed training camps. The new RAF camp was built in 1938-9, with later additions. First to arrive were 10 officers and 50 men in March 1939. By June the camp housed 1,700 trainees. The Technical Training School, RAF Hednesford, provided employment for many locals and mixed memories for those stationed there. The school lay on high ground just north of Hednesford, between Brindley Village and Marquis Drive. The gruelling trudge up 'Kitbag Hill' from Brindley Heath station must have dampened the spirits of

151 The Hednesford Home Guard in 1941. Winston Churchill wrote to the then Home Secretary in October 1941: 'Then what about all these people of middle age who served in the last war ... who are being told that they are not wanted ... Surely this is very foolish? Why not form a Home Guard?'

152 Moors Gorse pumping station, off the Rugeley Road, between Hednesford and Rugeley. A notable landmark for many years, although probably not a welcome sight for those who had to trudge up nearby 'Kitbag Hill' to the RAF Camp.

many a young recruit. The Chase was also used as a training ground for the Home Guard. In 1942 three members were killed by an exploding grenade in one episode on Hednesford Hills. Wartime restrictions meant that little was published about the tragedy. All sorts of bullets and shrapnel still litter the Chase and the occasional live piece turns up from time to time. Such was the danger in some parts that the main grenade range, near Milford, was out of bounds to the public until well after the war.

Tanks were manufactured at Stafford and tested on the Chase. General de Gaulle was photographed taking part in one of the exercises.

153 Harry Dutton, licensee of the *West Cannock Inn*, Hednesford. Mr. Dutton kept the pub for many years. As the inn was within walking distance of the RAF Camp, it no doubt provided a welcome break for many a trainee.

154 Street Party, Dartmouth Road, Cannock. The party was held near the junction of Longford Road. The lady in the striped dress is Mrs. Hanley. Inspector Heath is the gentleman wearing the chain. Michael and David Battersby are seated second and third right respectively.

155 Prefabs at Pye Green. These homes were erected in the years following the Second World War to meet the desperate shortage of accommodation across the country. The old Water Tower is in the background, which still stands today.

Apparently, damage to the western side of Old Acre Valley was evident thirty years after the war. Perhaps the keen-eyed could still make it out today? Major fires have also damaged the Chase from time to time. During the last war schoolboys worked through their holidays to make fire-breaks, supervised by their teachers. Lads from Littleworth Boys School made up one contingent. They worked long hours and walked miles each day. They were rewarded with extra, unofficial, rations. I have been told that some were heartily sick of venison stew by the end of the summer holidays.

Fortunately, the Chase escaped serious bombing raids. Some oil bombs fell near Heath Hayes in 1940; luckily there were no casualties. Most of the bombs which fell seem to have been those jettisoned by pilots getting ready to turn at Gailey Pools for the journey back to Germany. The ruins of fortified gun emplacements at Middle Hill can still be seen in a field alongside the Wolverhampton Road. One of the reasons why they were sited there was to pick off such planes. Sadly, tragic accidents are also part of war. At nearby Cheslyn Hay one local man, Clifford Hooper, can vividly recall an Allied aeroplane, a Boulton Paul Fighter on a training exercise, breaking up and crashing near Middle Hill in the summer of 1941.

Eventually the war ended and street parties celebrated VE and VJ days. Somehow film was found to photograph these events. Heroic and imaginative efforts were made to provide the best food and drink possible and rows of beaming faces smile at the cameras. For many of the young children it was probably the first time they had had their picture taken.

After the war the RAF school remained in use; most young men were expected to do national service until 1957. Within weeks of the last passing

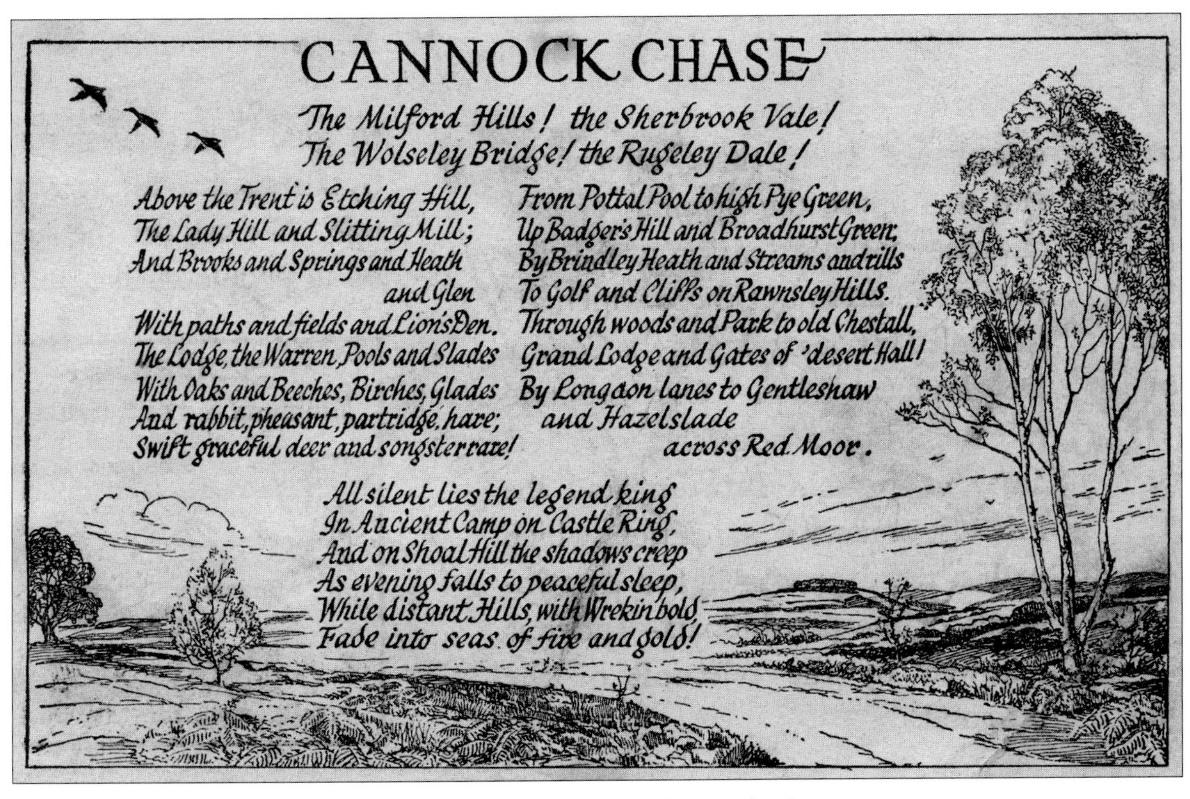

CANNOCK CHASE
The Milford Hills! the Sherbrook Vale!
The Wolseley Bridge! the Rugeley Dale!
Above the Trent is Etching Hill,
The Lady Hill and Slitting Mill;
And Brooks and Springs and Heath and Glen
With paths and fields and Lion's Den.
The Lodge, the Warren, Pools and Slades
With Oaks and Beeches, Birches, Glades
And rabbit, pheasant, partridge, hare;
Swift graceful deer and songster rare!
From Pottal Pool to high Pye Green,
Up Badger's Hill and Broadhurst Green;
By Brindley Heath and Streams and rills
To Golf and Cliffs on Rawnsley Hills.
Through woods and Park to old Chestall,
Grand Lodge and Gates of 'desert Hall!
By Longdon lanes to Gentleshaw
and Hazelslade
across Red Moor.
All silent lies the legend king
In Ancient Camp on Castle Ring,
And on Shoal Hill the shadows creep
As evening falls to peaceful sleep,
While distant Hills, with Wrekin bold,
Fade into seas of fire and gold!

156 An ode to the abiding beauty of Cannock Chase.

out parade in the autumn of 1956, the camp became home to 1,200 Hungarian refugees. They were some of the lucky ones who managed to escape after the failed rising against the Communists. Twenty-five thousand people died at the hands of Soviet troops and, with the Cold War at its height, there was a great deal of sympathy for Hungary. That first Christmas a big effort was made to welcome the refugees. I can remember my parents asking me to make up a box of my toys for the children at the camp. I regretted parting with my toy iron for months – goodness knows why, because I hate ironing now!

Today tourists can follow the 'Great War Trail' on the Chase or call in at the Visitors' Centre at Marquis Drive. I doubt whether anyone could have envisaged such a thing during either of the wars. Nearby, the Museum of Cannock Chase is dedicated to the preservation of the area's industrial history. Future histories of the Chase will, no doubt, explore the tremendous impact of leisure and tourism on the local economy. The new millennium appears to be heralding many changes. Who can say what is in store for Cannock Chase in the next thousand years?

Further Reading

General Titles

Greenslade, M.W., *A History of Cannock and Neighbourhood* (1982)
Hackwood, F.W.M., *The Chronicles of Cannock Chase* (1903)
Everitt, S.M., *Staffordshire Millennium Embroideries* (1999)
Pitman (M. Wright), *The Best of Cannock Chase* (1933)
Pitman (M. Wright), *The Friendship of Cannock Chase* (1935)

Specialist Titles

Benson, J. (ed.), *The Miners of Staffordshire* (1993)
Francis, R., *A Transport History of Cannock Chase* (1975)
Gammon, R.S., *Statesman and Schemer, William, First Lord Paget* (1973)
Godwin, J., *Beaudesert and the Pagets* (1982)
Linford, F., *The History of Cannock Conduit Trust* (1974)
Morris, J. (ed.), *Domesday Book: Staffordshire* (1976)
Whitehouse, C.P. and Ibbotson, G.P., *Great War Camps on Cannock Chase* (1978)
Whitehouse, C.P., *Kitbag Hill* (1987)

Autobiographies

Wakefield, Tom, *Forties Child* (1980)

Index

Figures in **bold** refer to illustration page numbers.